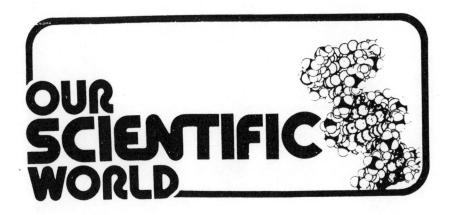

OUR SCIENTIFIC WORLD

Paul A. Bartz
Managing Editor

Barbara Johannes
Associate Editor

Bonnie J. Bartz
Design Editor

Wesley Chase
Contributing Editor

$\underline{B}$ ible
$\underline{S}$ cience
A ssociation

Kendall/Hunt
Publishing Company
Dubuque, Iowa

Copyright © 1986 by the Bible Science Association

Library of Congress Catalog Card Number: 85–82460

ISBN 0–8403–3869–4

Printed in the United States of America

B   403869   01

Table of Contents

For more information and additional teaching resources, all listed in our up-to-date catalog, free upon request, please write: The Bible-Science Association, 2911 East 42nd Street, Minneapolis, Minnesota, 55406.

ABOUT OUR SCIENCE READERS BOOKS

Throughout their history **Our Science Readers** have always had the very unique purpose of providing a positive and productive education for Christian children living in a culture which takes evolution for granted at every turn. Over the years the writers and editors of **Our Science Readers** have developed sound educational approaches to show young people in each age group that the Bible offers an intelligent alternative to evolution.

Even though young people may not be familiar with the word "evolution" until eighth grade, the concepts of evolution — an ancient earth, millions of years of history, and "horses once looked like this . . ." — are presented even to younger children. By the time they reach seventh grade students have been taught most of the fundamental concepts of evolution as fact, even though they have not been taught to recognize the word "evolution."

Even children in Christian schools are not protected from this subtle brainwashing. Many Christian schools use state-supplied textbooks, children watch television and listen to the radio and read. Every one of these forms of communication helps build the impression that evolution is scientific fact.

The topics offered in **Our Scientific World** are uniquely presented. Where else can you send a student to do research on coal, the Galapagos Islands, or petroleum in the confidence that he can do his research without having evolution subtly thrust into his thinking? And more importantly, **Our Scientifc World** supplies the student with important facts which help him see that the Biblical view is an intelligent and better alternative to evolution. The cross-referencing in this volume also allows a student to research the sub-parts of major topics, like the fossil record, or the Flood, in order to develop his topic on as wide a scope as desired. Such cross-referencing also helps the student to see how various topics are related to one another.

Knowing at just what point a child becomes sensitive to which evolutionary programming, as well as which grade levels stress which issues, our writers and editors offer this volume of **Our Science Readers Books** for grade seven. You will find that this volume offers the Christian child science lessons which are deeply rooted in the Biblical view of the world. This science is in the spirit of the founders of modern science who did more than develop the basis and principles of modern science. They developed science with a deep sense that our Creator is intimately involved in His creation, and He desires to be more intimately involved in our personal lives through His Son Jesus Christ.

There is truly no aspect of human existence where Jesus Christ does not belong. And the best way to show a child how to integrate God's love and will into all parts of his or her life is to show how He is truly Lord; yes, even in science!

To Him be the Glory!

      Paul A. Bartz
      Managing Editor
      Our Science Readers Books

ANTHROPOLOGY — TRACING OUR ROOTS

The Study of Man

More people are interested in what is happening now because "now" seems to have more meaning to us. But what we are doing now, and even who we are has a lot to do with the past. The past is very alive today in us!

We are products of our past. The world you live in was not shaped by you. It was shaped by your parents' generation, your grandparents' generation, and by people hundreds of years ago. To understand yourself, then, you need to know something of your family and past.

In the same way, if we want to know what people are, we must ask about the history of the human race. Where did human beings come from? How has human culture developed?

The Bible says that man was created a little lower than the angels, and in God's image. It tells us about how God has given us a Savior. Evolution says that man is an animal and we need no Savior.

ANTHROPOLOGY: WHERE DID HUMAN CULTURE COME FROM?

There is not a single field of study which has not been greatly changed by the concept of evolution: astronomy, geology, philosophy, ethics, religion, anthropology, and all others, Darwin applied his theory only to biology, but others thought evolution could be applied to all areas of human knowledge.

So evolution has been used to explain where human culture came from, too.

In Darwin's day evolutionary anthropologists looked upon "primitive" cultures as pictures of the early stages of their own society — as sort of "living fossils" showing where they evolved from.

Early Views of Culture

Anthropologists have said that there are steps through which societies supposedly pass. They have suggested that societies pass from savagery to barbarism, to militarism, to industrialism. Early evolutionists thought that their society was the highest of all the steps. They thought that the Bushman and the African black man were lower on the evolutionary ladder than the white man, placing them somewhere between apes and humans.

Evolutionists have tried to trace the evolutionary stages of all parts of society. They say that technology is supposed to have followed the pattern of wood, stone, bronze, then iron. In religion, the evolutionary development is said to be: magic, ancestor worship, polytheism (believing in many gods), and monotheism (believing in one God). The most advanced religion is concerned with morals.

The "Armchair" School of Anthropology

Does culture really progress in stages of development? Scientists today no longer believe it does, and have rejected this model of social evolution. The theories of nineteenth-century evolutionists were not based on actual observation of other cultures, but on wrong information and guesses. Theirs was an "armchair" school of anthropology, without firsthand experience.

Today, many anthropologists reject the evolutionary idea of stages altogether, believing instead in other models such as the dispersion model.

Old Ideas Don't Die Quickly

In the history of thought, a theory may be proven false and rejected, but the general idea remains in people's thinking. So it is with much of Darwin's own theory of evolution. And so it is with evolutionary anthropology. While ideas of how human culture supposedly developed have been rejected, the basic idea remains that man began primitive and brutish and pulled himself up by his bootstraps through stages of improvement.

Adam and Eve started the highest culture this earth has ever seen. The fall into sin not only made it impossible for us to do God's will perfectly, but it also changed human culture. For this reason creationists believe that good human culture needs the power of God in the Gospel active within the lives of people.

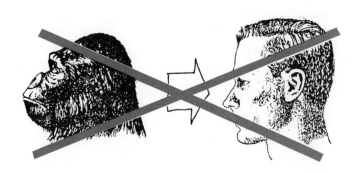

See also "Fossil Man"

Astronomy

Who hasn't looked at the night sky and stood in awe at the beauty of the stars? Nothing stirs our imaginations more than the thought of space. One question which always comes up is "Where did the stars and all the wonders we see in the sky come from?"

Was the universe created or has it always existed?

That question has always been interesting for man. The idea of a creation appears in the legends of many ancient peoples. They tell of gods or godesses who give the universe form, shaping it into the earth, the heavens, and the world of living things.

The question of the origin of the universe is really the question of where matter itself first came from. Both creation scientists and evolutionary scientists have tried to answer this question.

The Bible teaches that all matter was created out of nothing by God. This month we shall be looking at the scientific evidence which says that this is the only possible and truly scientific explanation for the origin of matter and the universe.

Matter — Eternal or Created?

The ancient Greeks thought that just as people and animals begin life as newborns, grow to maturity, age and die, so worlds pass through stages. The world is like a watch that slowly runs down until it can no longer continue. Then the gods step in and restore all things as they were at the beginning. These age-long cycles were thought to repeat themselves over and over endlessly.

At first science seemed to support the view that matter is eternal. A law of science called the Law of Conservation states that matter can neither be created nor destroyed. When this law was first learned, it seemed to many that science had dealt the death blow to belief in creation.

Of course only God is eternal. But those who reject the true God of the Bible want to find something else that is eternal to replace God. And so, many who favor evolution have suggested that matter is eternal. They believe that the same matter they think is eternal also created them. They have replaced the Creator with the creation, as Romans 1:25 warns us against.

THE SOLAR SYSTEM

Our sun is special among the stars of the universe. It is the only star in space that we have proven has planets.

Our solar system has many different types of objects. Besides the nine planets, there are dozens of moons, smaller chunks of rock called asteriods, and comets. The variety in the solar system is amazing. Some planets are so hot that lead would melt on them. Others are so cold and far away from our sun that the sun just looks like another bright star in the sky. All of this in addition to the variety and life which is found on earth!

This variety reveals the unlimited creativity and wisdom of God. He has also left many evidences in the solar system that He is its Creator. The exploration of space is bearing out the truth of what the Bible tells us.

THE AGING UNIVERSE

Look at any book on astronomy from your library and you will probably find a section entitled "the evolution of stars." Such a section will include a colorful diagram which is supposed to show the theory that stars evolve from bright burning blue, to large red, to tiny "white dwarf" stars.

Even though astronomers have searched the sky with telescopes for over 370 years, no one has actually seen the formation of new stars. Nor have astronomers seen one kind of star evolve into another kind. What *has* been seen are differences among stars: bright blue, dim red, small white, or yellow. But do these differences mean that the stars are evolving, or only that there is variety in the heavens? It depends upon one's understanding.

The Bible tells us that God *made* the stars, He did not *evolve* them. The whole creation tells of the amazing variety of God's creative genius and power!

Where Did the Solar System Come From?

According to evolutionary astronomers, the sun and planets condensed out of swirling, cold, dark clouds of gas and dust.

There is a major problem with this idea, according to Fred Hoyle, a modern evolutionary astronomer. How did the dust particles stick together? The theory says that there were tiny bits of dust flying through space, bumping and sticking together to form small globs of matter. As they grow, the blobs increase in gravity, attracting more and more wandering dust particles. Gravity causes the ball to condense and its temperature to rise until it becomes hot, and *presto!* we have the sun. On the edges of the cloud, smaller clouds of whirling dust also condensed to form the planets.

The idea that the dust particles will hold together when they bump is a problem. This is not what happens in dust storms. In fact, when things hit each other, they will blow each other apart! We need something to stick the dust together, according to Hoyle. What was it?

Too Much Time

Another problem with the dust cloud theory is that the rolling clouds of gas and dust must remain together during the entire time the planets are forming. This is because the planets all move around the sun in the same direction. One astronomer has pointed out that knowing the principles involved, it is hard to explain how these clouds could have been in existence for even 10 or 100 years.

What Do We See in the Solar System?

While many of the bodies in the Solar System move in the same pattern around the sun, this is not always the case. But some larger bodies of the solar system do not circle the sun in the same way that others do. The dust cloud theory would lead us to believe that all the planets revolve on their axis in the same direction as the others. But in reality, two of the nine planets spin backwards.

If the entire solar system was formed in one and the same process of a single dust cloud, then the sun, planets, and moons should all spin in the same way. Orbits should be pretty much the same.

Mind or Matter

It is hard to explain the origin of the solar system because we have never seen a system of planets form around a star. If we wish to come up with a theory of how it might have happened by looking backward into time, we find the barrier of the Second Law of Thermodynamics. The Second Law tells us that physical processes go in one direction only — downhill. Things don't get more orderly and gain more energy by themselves.

Creation scientists also believe that adding millions of years may make the theory seem more possible to many people. But millions of years don't help the globs of matter to collect into structured objects. In fact, adding more time makes it even more likely that the most natural process will win — which is decay.

Scientific findings about space agree with the Bible. Only a God could have made the solar system. How can you use this fact to tell others about God and His Son, your Savior?

THE SOLAR SYSTEM
(not to scale)

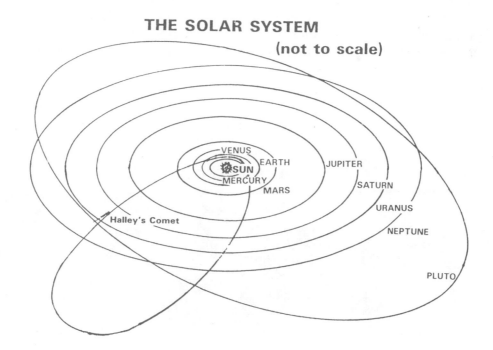

See also "Big Bang"

Big Bang

Something Bigger than the Big Bang

The most popular theory of the origin of the universe today is the "big bang" theory. According to the Big Bang theory, all the matter and energy in the universe was in a space smaller than the space taken up by a small atom today (the "big squeeze"). Then the ball exploded, throwing everything in all directions.

The Red Shift

When starlight passes through a prism, it breaks into a rainbow spectrum of colors. Black lines cut the spectrum in regular patterns. These black lines show the chemical elements in the star. The black spectral lines produced by distant stars and galaxies are not, however, in the positions expected for those elements. Instead the pattern of lines is closer to the red end of the spectrum — a "red shift."

The Doppler Effect

You have noticed how a train whistle sounds higher-pitched as the train comes towards you, and lower pitched as the train passes by you. Light does the same thing, except you can see a color change instead of hearing a sound change. So this red shift of the black lines is thought by some to be a Doppler effect. By the same principle, the side of the sun that is turning toward the earth shows a blue shift and the side that is turning away shows a red shift.

If the galaxies are flying away from each other now, then in the past they must have been closer. If we trace their paths back in time, at some time they must come together at a single point. The galaxies must have begun as a single ball of matter, so the argument goes.

THE DOPPLER EFFECT

SOUND WAVES STRETCHED

SOUND WAVES PUSHED TOGETHER

(LIGHT: RED SHIFTED)

(LIGHT: BLUE SHIFTED)

Needed: Something "Bigger" Than the Big Bang

Most evolutionary scientists accept the big bang theory because it is a totally natural explanation of the origin of the universe. And yet, it makes them a bit uneasy. According to well-known astronomer Robert Jastrow, an evolutionist, the reason scientists are disturbed by this theory is that it agrees with what creationists have believed all along. To believe that the universe had a beginning is to agree that there is a point at which natural science stops — its beginning is an event which the known laws of science cannot explain. Although not himself a creationist, Jastrow declares that, for all scientists really know, the cause may have been God.

Other theories on the origin of the universe have been offered to explain the beginning of the universe. Yet each of these theories have serious difficulties. A big part of the problem in coming up with a theory for the "evolution" from a gas cloud to a structured universe is the uphill nature of the process. According to physical laws as we know them, the universe in which we live is very unlikely.

If water does not naturally run uphill, you need to add something outside of the water — a pump. Since natural processes do not go "uphill" toward greater complexity by themselves, you need to add, as Jastrow suggests, something outside of the forces of the universe in order to explain the universe.

God has carefully designed the universe so people will find that they cannot explain the origin of things without Him. Scripture tells us that He has done this so that people will finally be drawn to Jesus as their Savior.

See also "Astronomy"

Coal

COAL

According to the evolutionists, most of the world's coal was formed about 300 million years ago. They say that at that time the whole world was like a tropical forest. Plants grew very quickly. As plants died, new ones rapidly grew up over them until whole sections of the earth's surface were a mass of plant materials.

Sometimes parts of this huge "forest" would get covered with sand and mud which washed down from mountains. The plant material was sealed away from the air before it could begin to decay.

Finally, the land sank under the sea where all of the plant material was completely buried by silt. The water kept out the air, so the plant material did not decay. Instead other chemical actions took place, changing the mass into what we call peat. Additional sediments collected over this mass squeezing out much of the water, and the result is what we today call *lignite* coal. As the pressures became greater, the sediment above the lignite hardened into sandstone and shale. More pressure on the lignite resulted in the formation of *bituminous*, or soft coal. Pressures from the movement of the earth's crust caused the bituminous coal to change into *anthracite*, or hard coal.

The evolutionists' explanation of the way in which coal and oil were formed over millions of years does not agree with the Bible's history. But we do know that these gifts of God were made from dead plants and animals which became buried.

GLOSSARY

LIGNITE: The softest kind of coal. It burns easily. Technically this is not usually considered coal.

BITUMINOUS: Soft coal. Formed from pressure on lignite.

ANTHRACITE: The hardest type of coal. Anthracite is a result of pressure and heat applied to BITUMINOUS coal.

FOSSIL: The remains of a once-living creature which have been turned to stone. The body parts of the creatures are replaced with minerals which have been dissolved in water.

CREATION AND HOW COAL WAS MADE

Creationists and evolutionists agree that coal was made from dead plants. But, creation scientists find it hard to believe that coal was formed mainly from vast peat bogs. It takes a peat bog ten feet deep to make a coal layer which is one foot thick. Many coal layers are 40 feet thick. This would mean that the original bog was 400 feet thick. Creation scientists point out that this is unlikely. Some of the great coal beds, such as the Appalachin coal basin, extend 70,000 square miles or more. No one has ever heard of a peat bog which is anywhere near this size.

Coal layers are usually found on top of layers of earth which could not support great amounts of plant growth. So it seems that the vegetation was transported into the area in some way.

The shape of coal layers witnesses to the power of the great Flood at the time of Noah. The fact that coal is found all over the world witnesses to the fact that the Flood was a worldwide Flood.

WHAT DOES THIS MEAN?

Creation scientists have studied coal. They now believe that coal is the result of a great worldwide flood. Creation scientists point out that the coal beds lie in the earth just like other rock layers which were made by a great worldwide flood.

We have already told you how evolutionists think that the coal came to be made. We will now present the way in which creation scientists think that coal was made.

Creation scientists agree that coal is made from plants which died and were buried. Because the plants were buried and the air could not get to them, they did not decay. Instead, the weight of the earth above, and heat, changed the plants into coal.

Creation scientists believe that the world was warm and tropical before the flood. This is because the earth was surrounded with a water vapor canopy. This canopy was like a thin cloud which you could see through. It went all around the earth. This canopy acted like the roof of a greenhouse. Plants in such tropical climates today grow at an amazing rate. Bamboos can grow as much as a foot a day.

Then the vapor canopy collapsed, and volcanoes erupted. Huge rivers of water flowed from beneath the earth.

Holy Scripture tells us why God caused all of this to happen. People were sinful and they would not hear God's Word. Noah preached about the Savior, and how people should turn away from sin. But people would not listen. So God sent the Flood.

Imagine the sky filled with huge waterfalls, many times the size of **any** known today. These huge rains dropped billions of gallons of water per second from miles high. At the same time great oceans of water gushed from beneath the earth. Water gushed so rapidly from beneath the oceans that even deep sea animals were lifted over the dry land. Fossils of these animals have been found in coal, far from the sea.

AN EXPOSED COAL SEAM AS IT LIES IN THE EARTH. *(Courtesy of the U.S. Geological Survey)*

The fountains beneath the continents were also opening, and there was a fearful mixing of all of this water with that falling from the sky.

The force of this water ripped the seas apart. The waters rushed so fast that trees, huge animals, and huge rocks were carried for hundreds of miles from where they had been before the flood. For the first weeks of the flood the whole surface of the earth was a boiling mass of mud and floating trees and other plants. Finally the waters began to quiet down.

The heavier rock material settled out first. The plant materials were not yet water-logged. They were floating in huge rafts. Currents would often bring these huge floating rafts into contact with one another, and they would join and form even larger rafts.

These giant rafts were sometimes thousands of miles across. They finally became water-logged and sank. Then they were covered by more rocks and dirt. The result is coal.

The Flood was a terrible disaster. But God used it to make the coal which is a blessing to us. God can always bring good things out of bad things.

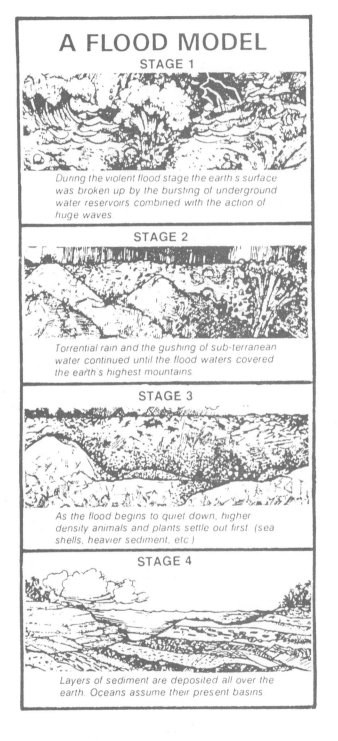

A FLOOD MODEL
STAGE 1

During the violent flood stage the earth's surface was broken up by the bursting of underground water reservoirs combined with the action of huge waves.

STAGE 2

Torrential rain and the gushing of sub-terranean water continued until the flood waters covered the earth's highest mountains.

STAGE 3

As the flood begins to quiet down, higher density animals and plants settle out first. (sea shells, heavier sediment, etc.)

STAGE 4

Layers of sediment are deposited all over the earth. Oceans assume their present basins.

INTERESTING FOSSILS IN COAL

Fossils are once-living things which were turned into rock. Fossils are like a picture of what things were like when the once-living thing was buried. Many fossils are found in coal. If evolutionists are right, there were no people living when the plants which are now coal were buried. If creation scientists are right we would not be surprised to find fossil bones of people in coal. Let's see what we find.

A lot of fossils of people and what they made have been found in coal. These discoveries are scientific evidence which calls evolution into question, say creation-scientists.

FOSSILS OF HUMANS IN COAL

One of the best known human finds in coal was the fossilized human skull found in Freiberg, Germany. This was found in 1842.

This fossil discovery is explained in detail in the book, **The Genesis Flood**, by Dr. Henry Morris, a creation scientist. A discovery like this—and there have been many—shows how the Bible's story of creation, man and history is correct, and evolution is wrong.

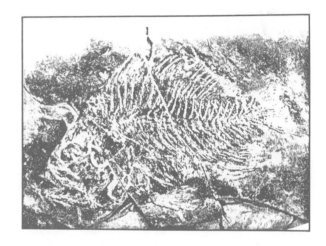

MANY FOSSILS LIKE THIS ONE ARE FOUND IN COAL.*(Courtesy of the U. S. Bureau of Mines.)*

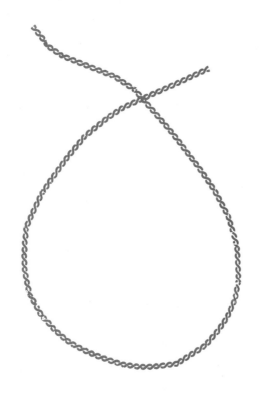

A MYSTERIOUS GOLDEN CHAIN

On June 9, 1891, Mrs. S. W. Culp of Morrisonville, Illinois was shoveling coal into her stove when a large lump broke open. Out fell a ten-inch long, eight carat gold chain. Reporters for the newspaper, the *Morrisonville Times* studied the chain and found that a lump of coal still hung on the chain, and the coal out of which it came still had the imprint of the chain. This coal was dated at 300 million years old by evolutionists. That is over one hundred times older than the first people were supposed to have evolved!

Christianity is more than just knowing the right history. These discoveries show how the Bible is right. But the purpose of the Bible is to tell us about our Savior Jesus. To trust Him for our salvation is the heart of our faith.

HUMAN FOSSIL IN

COAL

In 1958, Dr. Johannes Huerzeler of the Museum of Natural History in Basel, Switzerland, found a human jawbone in a coal mine in Tuscany, Italy. The jaw was of a modern person. It seemed to have belonged to a child of about five or seven years of age. The problem is that the coal layer from which the bone was removed is dated at 20 million years old. Dr. Huerzeler declared this to be the remains of the world's oldest man, but his fellow scientists generally ignored the whole thing.

A discovery of this sort is not surprising to those who know and believe what the Bible says about man. Man was made by God when the world was 6 days old. We are not surprised when the oldest rocks show us that people were living on earth from almost the beginning.

THESE CRINOIDS LIVE AS DEEP AS A MILE IN THE OCEAN. THEY ARE OFTEN FOUND FOSSILIZED IN COAL WHICH WAS FORMED FROM LAND PLANTS. SUCH FOSSILS ARE EVIDENCE OF A VIOLENT WORLDWIDE FLOOD. *(Courtesy of the Smithsonian Institution)*

LAND CREATURES MEET DEEP SEA CREATURES!

The fossilized bones of people and other modern creatures which live on the surface of the earth are not the only mysteries to be found in the coal beds. Evolutionists say that coal was formed on land. But many fossils of many deep sea creatures can be found in coal. Fossils of deep sea creatures called crinoids, "sea lilies" or "feather stars," which live very deep in the sea are often found mixed with the fossils of land creatures. This scientific evidence means that there was a great mixing of everything on the land with deep sea creatures when the coal beds were made.

Creation scientists believe that this great mixing happened when God brought the great Flood in Noah's time. Here we see more scientific evidence that evolution is wrong, and the Bible is right.

"OUT OF PLACE" FOSSILS IN COAL

These fossils and other objects have been found in coal. These are the kinds of objects creation science predicts *might* be found. Evolutionary science predicts that these objects *could not possibly* be found in coal because coal is too ancient to have these fossils in it.

MODERN HUMAN TOOTH — Bear Creek, Montana

MODERN HUMAN SKULL — West Germany

MODERN CHILD'S JAWBONE— Tuscany, Italy

IRON CUBE — Austria

GOLD CHAIN — Morrisonville, Illinois

IRON POT — Oklahoma

SOURCE: *Strange Relics from the Depths of the Earth, by J. R. Jochmans, Lit.D., Forgotten Ages Research Society, Lincoln, Nebraska. More complete documentation is included in this book which is available from Bible-Science.*

See also "Flood," "Fossil Record," and "Young Earth"

Design

THE APPEARANCE OF DESIGN IN LIVING THINGS

Mankind has always wondered at the appearance that nature has been designed. Both evolutionary and creation scientists have tried to answer this question.

The real puzzle is that there are so many things in nature which appear to be designed to work in very special ways. Things which look designed usually are designed.

Darwin's book, **Origin of the Species**, was published in 1859. Before the publication of the book most people were convinced that the order and complexity of the universe proved its creation by an intelligent being. But Darwin's ideas raised questions about the cause or causes in the universe.

Of course we know that the creation appears designed because it was designed by God. The basic argument for God from design says that if something cannot fall together by chance, it *must* have been designed. Not all evolutionists agree that evolution can explain the design in nature.

DESIGN OR CHANCE?
Can One Be Proven —
Disproving The Other?

Is there any way to disprove either the idea that nature has been designed by an intelligent Designer, or the idea that natural forces can explain the apparent design in nature? Darwin said that his explanation that things only *looked* designed because of natural selection *could* be disproven.

Darwin wrote that natural selection works by small changes, making new animals and new things in animals a little at a time. So, he said, if anyone could show how new animals or new parts of animals *could not* be formed a little at a time, "my theory would absolutely break down."

But there are many such examples. Many organs must exist in nearly perfect form before they are of any use at all. If only partly developed, they would be useless or even harmful. Consider the following examples.

The Wings of Bats and Birds

According to the theory of evolution, all creatures which fly evolved from animals that once ran upon the ground. Birds are said to be an evolution from reptiles. Bats are thought to have evolved from some creature similar to the mouse.

The Darwinian explanation of how bats evolved their wings, for example, is that the front feet changed slowly and gradually into wings. Each change wingward was preserved by natural selection because it was a help in the struggle for existence. It is more likely, however, that the opposite was the case. When the change was slowly taking place during thousands of years, it is doubtful the creature would manage to survive. The toes of the bat would slowly lengthen, and a thin skin would be stretched between them. During the many stages in between, the poor creatures had neither feet for running nor wings for flying. Their front legs would be useless, making it impossible for the creatures to either get food or escape from their enemies. They would be left to flounder about in a helpless fashion. The entire species would have perished long before the wings became complete. (No fossils of this vast, gradual change from four-footed animals to winged creatures are found anywhere in the fossil record. Bats appear in the fossil record fully formed and identical to modern bats.)

Interrelationships

A symbiotic relationship is one in which two living things are completely unable to live without the other. How, then, did the one survive the millions of years required for the other to develop? How did each live through the totally helpless stage until they evolved their dependent relationship? The classic example is the yucca plant and the yucca moth, which we will look at later.

Can Chance Produce Design?

Examples of this kind could be listed for pages and pages. One famous evolutionary scientist listed seventeen important features which cannot be explained by Darwinian selection and mutation.

Every evolutionary step in the formation of a new creature or a new feature must help the creature in some way because natural selection is a blind process. As another evolutionary writer said, natural forces cannot "plan ahead."

Evolution, besides being against the Bible, is not even good science, as we see here. Evolutionists have a hard time explaining the design in the creation when they have done away with the great Designer — God Himself.

Mammalian Ear Bones

It is thought that the reptile's jaw hinge bones gave rise to the bones of the middle ear of mammals. How did reptiles eat while the bones of their jaws were migrating through their skull to form the bones of the ear?

Instincts

The instincts of insects and animals defy any evolutionary explanation. The cells in the honeycombs of bees are marvels of design. In 1859, Darwin wrote to a Professor Miller about some measurements of the cells made by bees, "Your letter turned me sick with panic." At other times he said he "felt sick" when he thought of an eye or of a feather in the tail of a peacock knowing that he could not explain these things by his theory of natural selection. He would have felt even worse if he knew, as we now do, that bees can fly by an indirect route, and yet find the true direction without the aid of ruler or compass.

The migrating ability of animals is also a marvel. Birds find their way over long distances, and return to their nesting places. They can do this even if they have been moved thousands of miles from their nesting grounds. Even young birds, which have never before been away from the nesting area, fly to the wintering ground of their species.

The Human Eye

A good example of design is the human eye. The structure of the human eye led Darwin and others to question whether the problem of apparent design in living things can be explained by natural forces. Picture the eye evolving, step-by-step, through small changes which may be separated by millions of years. If even the slightest thing is wrong with the eye, if a part is missing, or it doesn't work right, or if something is the wrong size, the eye is useless. Since it must be either perfect, or perfectly useless, how could it have evolved by small, successive, Darwinian steps?

One evolutionist offers an answer. By choosing examples of living animals, he creates a series from the merely light-sensitive eyes of oysters to the excellent eyes of humans and birds. However, Macbeth (another evolutionist) says that this series has nothing whatever to do with how the human eye actually developed historically. There is no evidence at all that the members of this series are actually related to one another by evolutionary descent. Collecting a group of samples actually increases the problem of explanation: if we cannot explain how even one kind of eye came into existence naturally, it will be even harder to explain *several* kinds of eyes.

The created world which everyone sees every day still puts the lie to any evolutionary explanation. Countless organs and instincts could only have come about all at once, fully formed, by the sudden creation of an all-wise God. This can be our beginning point for bringing people to the knowledge of His love toward us in the Gospel.

19

The Eye and the Camera

You can compare the eye with a camera. They both have the same parts. One evolutionary scientist said that this must surely mean that both the eye and the camera are meant for the same purpose.

Since the camera was designed, we are stuck with the conclusion that someone or something must have designed the eye, says this scientist.

When we see that living things have a purpose which explains them, and we see how they are like the things which people design, we can understand how so many scientists have been led to believe that nature has been designed with a purpose in mind.

The "Machines" Of Life

Living beings are like designed machines. To grow and multiply, thousands of actions must be carried out within the cells of a living thing. Many different kinds of chemical reactions go on. These reactions are carefully controlled and timed by other chemicals. The cell is like a tiny factory, with chemicals acting as the machines that cut, weld, move, and change molecules.

Using only water, many kinds of bacteria take salts, simple sugars, and out of them make complex chemicals which we cannot make in our finest laboratories. All of this happens within the small single cell, too small to be seen with the naked eye.

It is easy to see that the machines that people make are designed by the use of thinking. In fact, human thinking is the only known explanation for the fact that machines do what they are supposed to do. So, creationists conclude that living things must also be the result of someone's thinking. Thinking must not only be within the human mind but also outside our material world.

As Scripture clearly says, Romans 1:20, God has filled the creation with signs of His eternal power and Divine nature. His wisdom and skill can be seen everywhere we look. The reason He has done this is so that seeing God's work we might be drawn to His greatest work which is our salvation.

PEOPLE DESIGN MACHINES BUT...

WHERE DID "MACHINES" IN NATURE COME FROM?

Can living things in nature be compared to human inventions? Is the design which we find in nature *of the same kind* as the design which we find in man's inventions? If design in man's machines can be compared to apparent design in nature, then we should be able to compare their sources.

As we examine some of the "machines" or "devices" of nature you can decide for yourself.

Man's inventions often turn out to be copies of things in nature. Man's inventions are designed, and still often don't work as well as things in nature. For this reason many have been led to believe that not only are the structures in nature designed, but they have been designed by a master Designer.

We know from the Bible that this master Designer is God Himself. From the care He has given to the things in nature we learn that He is not only concerned with the spiritual side of things, but He is *also* concerned about the material side of the creation. This important lesson will help keep us from thinking that God is only concerned about the spiritual things in life.

dreds of years before the first airplane flew.

The Secrets of Strong, Light-Weight Design

Methods which we use to build bridges, towers, cranes, airplanes, and so on can also be found in nature. In rushes, in straw, and in the bones of birds we find that the greatest strength can be had by the use of a hollow stem or tube, enabling the plant or bone to withstand side pressure. In the same way, *hollow tubes* are used in things like the bicycle to make it strong, but light.

In plants, the hollow stem is built of bundles of strong fibers on the outside which, weight for weight, may withstand as much weight as steel. Inside is a weak filling material which is filled with small air spaces, which helps it to withstand squeezing. When a reed bends in the wind both the strength of the fibers and the ability to be squeezed help the reed to keep from breaking.

Common Inventions

Many of the simple devices we use in everyday life have their counterparts in nature. The *lever* systems found in scissors are found in many creatures, a good example being the claws of crabs. The *lubrication* we use in all our machinery is like the lubrication of all moving parts in nature. Modern *gliders* work by picking out the rising currents of air, a trick used by the gossamer spider and, in ancient times, by the pterodactyl. *Streamlining* is a principle used by birds, insects, and fishes.

The same idea is used in the wings of airplanes to make them very light, yet very strong.

The "*stiffeners*" used in the great twelve-foot-thick supports of many bridges are very much like those found in plants. The tendency to "buckle" was resisted by the use of stiffener *rings* — set twenty feet apart within the tube—as in the jointed stem of the bamboo.

Flight

Early inventors studied the pattern of flight in birds very carefully. Leonardo da Vinci, for example, wrote that a bird obeys laws when it flies. He said that man could learn to build machines to do the same thing. This was hun-

God's goodness does not stop with our salvation which makes us new creations in Christ. It seems that He has filled His creation with ideas and designs to help make us able to carry out His command to subdue the earth. The most successful creation scientists use these ideas which God has already proven.

Follow the Pattern Provided

In Joseph Paxton's design of the Crystal Palace for the Great Exhibition of 1850, he copied the methods used in the huge leaves of the lily. "Nature was the engineer," he said. He said that he had copied the design of the lily so that his building would have both strength and beauty.

A few years ago, the Russians invented a "*mechanical mole*" for tunnel making. It works by copying the mole's method of pushing the earth at the back, and hardening the sides of the tunnel and cutting down the need to do a lot of digging.

The heart and the pump have been known to be a lot alike since the early days of science. Because of this the first real working modern pumps were made.

The principles used in *radar* can be found in nature. The bat sends out high sound waves and then picks up the echoes. He measures the time that passes before the echo returns, so he can tell the distance of the objects in its area. This works so well that bats can fly blindfolded between a series of wires which cross and re-cross a room.

Throughout history man has obtained most useful *drugs* from plants. This has helped us make a lot of the life-saving drugs we use today.

God invented and used these ideas first. We have just learned to discover them and copy them. Can you think of a problem which could be solved by searching for God's solution to the same problem in nature?

See also "Giraffe," "Life," and "Woodpecker"

Dinosaurs

DINOSAURS —
THEIR
STRANGE
PAST

What do you think of when you hear the word, "dinosaurs"? Is it a picture of a gigantic monster with big teeth, stomping around squashing houses like you see on TV movies? What do you really know about them? What have you been told? What have you read? This month we want to think about the dinosaurs and try to sort out facts and separate them from evolutionary ideas about these beasts.

Most people know three things about dinosaurs: they were big, dumb, and ugly; they lived millions of years ago; and they all died out and are extinct. You are entitled to believe the first item, but the second and third are open to question. We want to look at dinosaurs both from a science viewpoint and from a Bible viewpoint, and put what we learn together so that it makes sense. We do not believe some of today's scientific ideas about dinosaurs to be correct.

If you ask people when dinosaurs lived, you are nearly certain to get "millions of years ago" for an answer. Evolutionists have been able to sell this idea to the scientific community and to the public. Their plan has been so successful, people automatically think about dinosaurs as having lived millions of years ago. The idea that there might not have even BEEN millions of years ago shocks them.

The evolutionary ideas about dinosaurs are presented as fact everywhere. It's in school texts, on TV, in school science classes and films, in magazines and newspapers — even on school milk cartons. The message is the same: dinosaurs lived millions of years ago; they evolved; and they died out mysteriously.

We want to look at what is known and believed about dinosaurs. The name "dinosaur" is made out of two Greek words, "dinos" meaning terrible, and "sauros" meaning lizard, although dinosaurs are not considered lizards by scientists. The name was invented by an Englishman, Sir Richard Owen, about 1841.

Not much was known about dinosaur remains until the 1800's. This is when man invented steam shovels that could do serious deep digging. So modern science has been working with dinosaur skeletons for a little over 160 years. Following is a picture of what scientists think the "age of dinosaurs" was like.

Evolution theory says that the dinosaurs were the main kind of animal on the earth during a time called the Mesozoic Era. This, evolutionists say, started about 225,000,000 years ago and ended about 65,000,000 years ago. This is a span of time of about 160,000,000 years. This period is split into about three nearly equal divisions, named the Triassic, Jurassic, and Cretaceous periods. Dinosaurs "appear" in the late Triassic, and suddenly and completely disappear after the late Cretaceous, for reasons that puzzle scientists.

Most people think of dinosaurs as huge monsters, but many were small, or medium sized. The smallest one was the size of a pigeon, and others were chicken and turkey sized, and some were about dog and horse size. It is true a few types grew to 20 to 30 feet tall, and weighed from 60 to 85 tons or more! They were the largest *land* animals that ever lived. The largest animals ever are still with us, the whales.

There were two main types of dinosaurs, as classified by their pelvic bones: the "lizard-hipped" and the "bird-hipped" types. Some were four-legged types, and some stood erect and walked on two legs. Scientists believe (generally) that the earliest ones were small two-legged types, and that these evolved into all the other kinds. Creationists do not believe this because there are no in-between kinds of dinosaurs to show who evolved from what or how.

There were many kinds of body forms and sizes within the two main classes. Some were plant eaters, and some were meat eaters. You can tell by the structure of their teeth. Some had scales on their skin, some had bony armor plate all over them. Some had bills like a duck, but the bill was full of rough, flat teeth. Triceratops looked like an oversized rhinoceros with a big armor plate on his head with three big horns sticking out of it. Tryannosaurus Rex (the name means "king of the tyrant lizards") stood upright on two huge rear legs, and he had a five-foot head, with teeth six inches long filling his mouth. You wouldn't want to meet him in the dark. Probably not in the daytime, either. The kinds of dinosaurs seem to go on and on, and we have to wonder why there are so many kinds of them. Why would so many kinds evolve? Where are their ancestors? Why are they so different? God created them because He wanted to. He apparently had His own reasons for making them the way He did, even if we think them strange.

One strange dinosaur was Dimetrodon. He had a big fan-like sail right down his back from head to tail. Maybe you have seen pictures of him — most encyclopedias have them. Scientists have wondered what the big sail was for. Some thought it was to scare other animals as it was flipped up or down. But others thought it might be a kind of radiator, to help Dimetrodon regulate his body temperature. Reptiles, as we know them, are cold-blooded, which means they cannot control their internal body temperature. They must get their heat from their surroundings. So some scientists have suggested that the dino-

saurs may have been warm-blooded, like the mammal (like us). A big debate has raged over this. But it was all caused by evolutionary belief. Evolutionists believe all these structures must have some purpose that helps the animal survive. But Dimetrodon's sail stumped them. So they thought up this warm-blooded idea. But this raises more questions than it answers. If Dimetrodon was warm-blooded and needed the sail to keep cool, what about the other dinosaurs? What did THEY do to control THEIR temperature? The whole thing seems like a lot of overheated evolutionary imagination!

We mentioned before that scientists think dinosaurs evolved. You may find charts in books showing how this is thought to have happened. But we also mentioned that there are no dinosaurs that seem to be middle-way between one kind and another. They are all like each other within their types, just like animals today! Big ones do not have to be evolved from smaller ones. Besides, if bigger were better, why would the smaller types have survived? (They did.)

HERE YOU CAN SEE THE THICK LAYER OF ROCK WHICH MUST BE REMOVED TO FIND FRESH FOSSIL FOOTPRINTS OF HUMANS AND DINO-SAURS. YOU CAN SEE THE PALUXY RIVER IN THE BACKGROUND. (*Photo courtesy of Dr. Carl Baugh.*)

DINOSAURS — WHY DID THEY DISAPPEAR?

The greatest mystery about the dinosaurs is how and why they suddenly disappeared toward the end of the Mesozoic (so-called). Many articles mention this problem. They almost apologize for science's lack of a good answer. One encyclopedia says:

"All dinosaurs were extinct by the end of the Cretaceous period. None survived that time and no dinosaur can be alive anywhere today."

This seems to us a little too sure and confident. They may have to eat their words in a few years. More on that later.

Another encyclopedia admits:

"There is, however, no really satisfactory explanation for the sudden and complete extinction of the most spectacular animal fauna the Earth has ever known."

So scientists set about inventing explanations for the dinosaurs' extinction. All sorts of ideas have been proposed. Changes of climate, not enough food, mysterious diseases, their eggs devoured by mammals, rise of mountain chains with draining of swamps have all been considered. But it is unlikely that any of these things by itself would affect so many animals or on a worldwide scale. Lately, more ''scientific'' (science-fiction?) ideas like collision of the earth with an asteriod, or spraying the earth with radiation from an exploding star have been given as causes. Evolutionists are admitting that what happened to the dinosaurs must have been a worldwide catastrophe, because they were all killed off at about the same time. But these ideas cannot be proven, although there is plenty of evidence the earth suffered a great catastrophe in its past.

A clue to what really happened to the dinosaurs is found in the type of rock that contains their bones. It is called sedimentary rock, since it was deposited by water. It is formed by hardening the sand, silt and sediment that settles out of waters. It hardens chemically and by drying out, like concrete hardens to make a sidewalk. Can you figure out what happened? The dinosaurs' bones are often found in great masses. They are often mixed up, sometimes crushed and packed together. They are often twisted up into shapes suggesting agonizing death. Their bones are not broken or gnawed on by scavengers. What happened? They drowned or were buried alive in mudslides. A huge flood is the only thing that explains all the facts about how their bones are found.

By now you have surely found the key. The great Flood of Noah, as recorded in the Bible, could do all this. It fits all the facts. But it doesn't fit all the opinions and likings of some people, especially if they don't want to believe the Bible. Still, the evidence is there, and scientists are taking another look at the idea of

THIS WOODEN-HANDLED HAMMER WAS FOUND IMBEDDED IN ROCK NEAR LONDON, TEXAS. THE ROCK WAS DATED BY EVOLUTIONISTS TO JUST ABOUT THE TIME THAT THE FIRST LAND CREATURES WERE EVOLVING, AND SO THEY CANNOT ACCEPT IT AS BEING AS OLD AT THE ROCK. RECENT LABORATORY ANALYSIS FOUND THE IRON HEAD TO HAVE BEEN MANUFACTURED BY AN ADVANCED PROCESS. LAB TESTS ALSO SHOWED THAT BOTH THE ROCK AROUND THE HAMMER AND THE WOODEN HANDLE OF THE HAMMER HAVE SEEN GREAT PRESSURES — THE SORT WHICH WOULD FORM THE ROCK, AND PARTIALLY TURN THE WOODEN HANDLE TO COAL! (*Photo courtesy of Dr. Carl Baugh.*)

world catastrophe.

Two objections to the flood idea usually come up. (1) Evolutionists say that man and dinosaurs lived millions of years apart, and (2) Noah could not have had dinosaurs on his Ark. We will look at (1) now and (2) in the next article.

There is very good physical evidence that men and dinosaurs lived together at the same time. There are human and dinosaur footprints in Cretaceous limestone in the bed of the Paluxy River in Texas. Both had to be made when the limestone mud was still soft, like wet cement. They had to be made within days of each other, or weeks at most. The human tracks are very convincing. They have all the details and features they should have. Nobody questions the dinosaur tracks. They are real. But evolutionists cannot admit that man and dinosaur lived at the same time, or it will wreck their theory. And they might lose their jobs.

There are other fossil footprints in other places besides the Paluxy River, and they are also too old to be ''right.'' And there is a drawing of a dinosaur on a canyon wall made by an Indian in Arizona. Why would an Indian draw a picture of a dinosaur? If dinosaurs were extinct, he couldn't have seen one. And the drawing was probably made before white men settled the area, so he couldn't have heard about evolution. The simple answer is that he *saw* the dinosaur, despite what modern scientists think or believe.

Dinosaurs are not too much of a problem for the Biblical, scientific creationist. If the Creation account in Genesis is taken at face value, most dinosaurs were created on the sixth day, somewhat before man. So dinosaurs are older than man, but only by hours instead of millions of years. Men and dinosaurs lived together before the Flood, and very likely for some time after as well. They may still be around.

We mentioned the Paluxy River tracks before. Brontosaurus tracks and those of some three-toed dinosaur are there, and are undisputed. Evolutionists have claimed the man tracks are carved or that they are erosion marks made by the water. Both these claims are silly. The tracks run from the river bed up the bank and disappear under 8 to 10 feet of overlying rock and soil. When stripped away by bulldozer, the tracks continue. Who would

THESE FOOTPRINTS, THE HUMAN ON THE LEFT AND THE DINOSAUR ON THE RIGHT, HAVE JUST BEEN DISCOVERED. THEY WERE FOUND AFTER A THICK LAYER OF ROCK WHICH CAN STILL BE SEEN ON BOTH SIDES OF THE MEN WAS REMOVED. THESE HUMAN AND DINOSAUR FOOTPRINTS ARE ONLY SEVEN-AND-A-HALF INCHES APART. (*Photo courtesy of Dr. Carl Baugh*).

and could carve a whole trail of footprints? With perfect details? How would you do it in between the rock layers? The idea that the tracks are really erosion marks is even sillier. Would water carve separated marks in human-stride pattern? With details of arch and heel and mud push-up between the toes? What do you think? But the real shocker is that some of the tracks are GIANT-size tracks, about 16 to 18 inches long! That fits a man about eight feet tall, weighing about 400 pounds! and we think our football players today are big!

But you should know that giants were common in the early world. There are fossils of giant dragonflies, giant snails, and of course some dinosaurs were giants. And the Bible remarks in Genesis 6:4 about "giants in the earth in those days." Scholars disagree about its meaning, but the fossil record is not lacking in giants. So giant men should not be so surprising. Another interesting thing. Near to the Paluxy area the skeleton of a young Indian woman was found. She has been named the Panther Creek woman. And she was *seven feet* tall! This goes in good scale with our big fellow who made the Paluxy tracks. Tall Texans indeed!

We now want to deal with some other objections usually raised against the idea of Noah's Flood. Aside from its miraculous start by God Himself, critics often laugh at the idea of Noah having dinosaurs inside the Ark. A 60-ton brontosaurus would go right through the floor! And what would he eat? Noah would have to have a whole shipload of food just to keep the dinosaurs happy. This sounds like a tough argument, until you start to think. And God does. The answer is simple. God sent *young, small* dinosaurs to Noah. Easy to manage, easy to feed. Probably they were no bigger than a big dog or a small horse. And during the Flood year it is likely that the animals went into a state of hibernation, a sort of coma, and perhaps had to be fed only very occasionally. This is known to happen to animals under shocking conditions. They do not behave as they usually do. And remember, God could make them behave any way He wanted. After all, He created them all. Look up and read Genesis 18:14.

Another thing usually brought up about man and dinosaurs living at the same time is the idea that the dinosaurs were so huge and fierce they would eat the men and *we* would be extinct. This sounds sort of believeable, but again, there are things you need to consider.

First, dinosaurs were dumb. Their brains were very small for their body size. They would be easy to fool, easy to avoid. They would operate by instinct and reflex, as many reptiles do today. Men were quick and smart and understood dinosaur behavior and stayed out of the way of the big ones. And it may be that when some of them turned to eating meat (originally *all* animals were plant eaters, see Genesis 1:29-30), God gave them instincts to attack and eat only their own kind. This makes sense, since it would control their population. In addition, God placed fear of man into *all* the animals after they got off the Ark. (Genesis 9:2). This would include the surviving dinosaurs. Even today, wild animals, though they are physically stronger than man, are instinctively afraid of him, and have to learn not to be afraid. This God-given instinct is still in them. There is no evolutionary reason why this should be so.

THIS HANDPRINT, FOSSILIZED AS THE ROCK HARDENED, WAS DISCOVERED NEAR THE PALUXY RIVER IN TEXAS. IT WAS FOUND WITH HUMAN FOOTPRINTS AND VERY NEAR A DINO-SAUR FOOTPRINT. THIS IS EVIDENCE THAT HUMANS AND DINOSAURS ONCE LIVED AT THE SAME TIME ON THE EARTH. *(Photo courtesy of Dr. Carl Baugh.)*

HERE A HAND IS FITTED OVER THE FOSSILIZED HAND-PRINT IN THE SAME POSI-TION AS THE HAND THAT MADE THE PRINT. *(Photo courtesy of Dr. Carl Baugh.)*

See also "Fossil Record" and "Flood"

Ecology

What is it?

CARING FOR GOD'S GIFT OF THE EARTH

Do you know what the word "ecology" means? It has become a household word within the past decade or so, but still many people are a little confused about it and misuse it. They talk of "damage to the ecology" when they mean damage to environment or to living things. Ecology comes from "*oikos*" in Greek which means house or home, and the "ology" ending means "study of," as it does in so many names of the sciences. So ecology is the "study of the home" or more accurately, the study of plants and animals in *their* homes.

No living thing is self-sufficient. Plants and animals depend on each other and on their non-living surroundings to give them the essentials of life. Plants are the basic food-providers for all animals. This means that plants are at the bottom of food chains. Plants can change water, carbon dioxide and sunlight into stored energy in the form of sugars and starches, with the help of their remarkable green "magic stuff," chlorophyll. Exactly how this happens is still not entirely understood. Animals that eat the plants are called herbivores. These animals give off wastes that the plants use as fertilizer to help them grow. Other animals that eat animals (carnivores) are getting plant food "second hand" when they eat an herbivore. This goes on and on in "food chains" or "pyramids." The animals also use oxygen that the plants give off, and the plants use the carbon dioxide that the animals breathe out. Neat, isn't it?

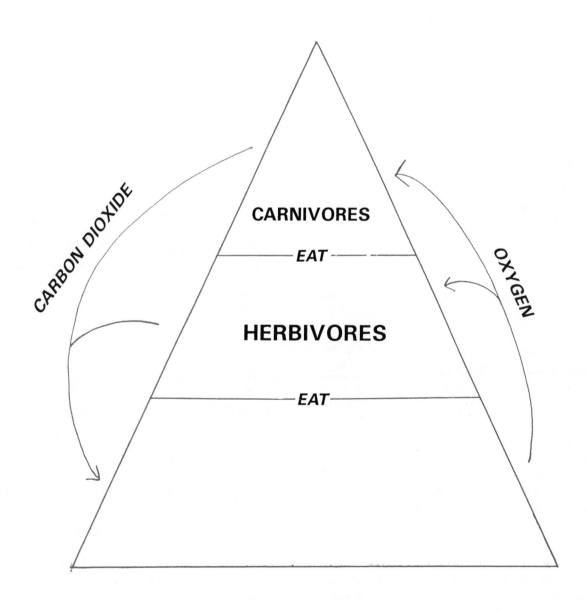

Can you believe these complex relationships that help each other just evolved accidentally? How would the animals and plants survive to become a balanced system if these things were not yet worked out? Dying is a great deal simpler than surviving. Yet scientists today (most, but not all) rather thoughtlessly accept the notion that all these systems just happened by the chance of evolution over millions of years. But the more you know about ecology, the harder that idea is to believe.

There are two main kinds of ecology, pure and applied. Pure ecology just studies "natural" situations and relationships. It studies where animals live, what they eat, how they reproduce, their populations and where they live. There is a lot to study, as you might guess. Applied ecologists study situations that are problems for man. Examples of applied ecology wuld be the use of knowledge to control insects and disease in crops, how to get better harvests, or how to avoid effects of pollution. Applied ecology is trying to "help nature along" — at least to the profit of man, but often to the benefit of animals and plants as well.

Did you know that nature also creates pollution of its own.? The swamps of the world, along with decaying organic matter, produce more carbon monoxide than all of man's factories and automobiles put together, in fact, more than ten times as much![1] But there is a difference. Natural pollutants can be broken down by sunlight and oxygen into harmless products that are recycled. Man-made chemicals are often new forms of matter which cannot be broken down by natural organisms or forces. One example is plastics. They contaminate the earth and remain indestructible, or nearly so.

Volcanoes, if you think about it, produce large amounts of air pollution and solid pollu-

tants. The recent eruption of Mt. St. Helens showed this. "Nature" as it now is, is neither harmless nor wholly good, as some people seem to think.

Pollution problems caused by man have been around since the 1600's, when the Industrial Revolution began and man began burning lots of fossil fuels (coal, oil, natural gas) to provide the energy to run newly invented machines. At first, the harm of many forms of pollution were unknown. But when they were discovered, the real problem was that few people cared. The natural system can clean itself up and correct some amounts of pollution. But man's industrial activities have gone so fast and on such a large scale that nature cannot cope. And now the results are coming and we *have* to worry about the problem.

34

First, the Bible teaches Creation *ex nihilo* — which is Latin, meaning ''out of nothing.'' This shows God's power (man cannot do this). It gives meaning and purpose to the material world — it is not just ''stuff'' — God made it, personally. The early Church had a hard time with false teaching based on Greek philosophy. One of these teachings was that matter is evil. But the Bible teaches that the physical and chemical world was made by God Himself, through His Son. See John 1:1-3.

God's own opinion of His work is found in Genesis 1 where the phrase ''and God saw that it was good'' is repeated six times in the creation story. Interestingly, most of these judgments *come before* the creation of human beings, who were made last. So nature is good in and of itself, with or without man. Animals and plants glorify God just by being, not just by their usefulness to man. In fact, there are many plants and animals that seem to be of no use at all to man. What good to man are penguins or poisonous mushrooms? What good are giraffes or tarantulas?

First, science and technology by themselves are not so much responsible for pollution as selfish and thoughtless people. Do we need to have wars? Do we really need everything that is made of plastic? Secondly, it appears that *most* of the scientists and manufacturers in the past and even the present are not practicing Christians. Probably most of them in these times are evolutionists.

As Christians, we have to make a distinction between the *historical* record of

what Christians have done and what the Bible teaches. There is no question that there has been a huge gap between these two many times. But it does not make sense to blame the Bible for man's failure to believe and follow it.

Man was created last, of the "dust of the ground," Genesis 2:7. But man was the crown of God's creation and was to have dominion (rulership) (Genesis 1:26) over all other life forms because man was made in God's image. This means, among other things, that man can have spiritual fellowship with God in ways animals cannot.

But man is not a divine being by himself. He is mortal and dwells in an earthly, material body that is very dependent on his environment, including plants and other animals. Pollution has only emphasized man's need for the rest of creation. The Bible does not teach that man is the center of all things. This idea is the root idea of *humanism*, which makes man the measure of all things.

Man was created and placed in the Garden of Eden to "till and keep it." The word "till" in Hebrew is the root word for "serve" or "to be a slave to." The word "keep" in Hebrew means to "watch" or "preserve." Notice that the words describe action done not for the benefit of man, but for the benefit of the creation. Keeping of the garden was not done just for Adam and Eve's comfort, but to preserve it, as a service to it and to God. Man is to be a keeper of nature as well as of his fellowmen. So Adam and Eve were stewards or managers of their surroundings. They had no license to kill, spoil or destroy. Their authority over the world was given to them by God. But what they were to do was to be in the limits of God's will for all of the creation.

We need to understand what ''progress'' means. Christians need to show that spiritual values are real and better than the endless production and consumption of ''junk'' that has been so much a part of our culture. Luxury and waste can be seen as sins in a Christian framework, but evolution has nothing to say about such matters. And such matters control the destiny of the country on pollution-ecology issues.

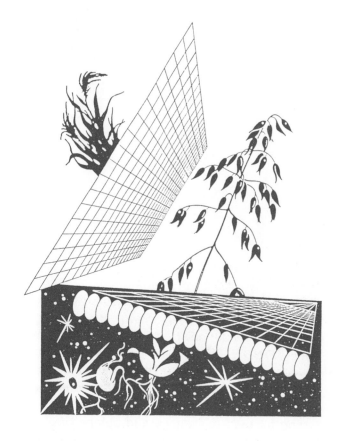

What about the future? Will things get better or worse? Probably some of both. There are those who think science and technology will get us out of our messes, but they are forgetting that it was these two that helped us get into them, and that the answers involve moral questions that science cannot solve. Technology is creating problems as fast or faster than it is solving them. Things may get worse before they get better. People do not want to face the huge cost in money and effort and changes of values that cleanup will involve. Those who are looking for humanist (man-centered) solutions from an evolutionary viewpoint are going to be disappointed. Evolutionists cannot come up with reasons why man should respect the rest of the living world. If evolution produced it all by accident,

Most people fall into two groups. There are the happy optimists who think that science will solve our problems, and there are those who are in despair over the possibility of doing so. The truth is somewhere in between. Albert Schweitzer once said: "Man has lost the capacity to foresee and forestall. He will end by destroying himself." · This dismal view might be true except for God's grace. From Biblical prophecy we learn that although man will pass through dark tunnels of trouble, there is light at the end and that light is the return of Jesus Christ.

God will not allow mankind to totally destroy himself, and Christ's return will climax human history and close the books on human suffering, poverty, mismanagement, war, disease, famine and misery. The book of Revelation promises a new heaven and a new earth, eventually. It is a grand promise and a winning situation for those who are on God's side. Man's problems will finally be solved, but not by man or his science. God has promised He will "make all things new," Revelation 21:5. It is this hope that sustains the Christian and quiets his soul in troubled and polluted times. The ecology of the future is Eden restored.

is man any better adapted or adjusted than a grasshopper? But deep down, they know better. Evolutionists *REASON LIKE CREATIONISTS* when it comes to environment questions. They even refer to animals as "creatures," not "evolutioners" — have you noticed that? They know it is wrong for man to damage and deface God's handiwork, but they don't know why because they do not acknowledge that God made it. But we will remind them.

Pollution is not the only problem man has to face and not the most pressing one. War itself is an expression of "spiritual pollution" due to man's fallen nature and Satan's activity.

Like it or not, man will have to accept the idea that almost *all* of his activities result in some form of environmental change, some of it harmful. All animals live at the expense of their environment and each other. The living world is organized into food chains and cycles. All this is carefully balanced and runs under the rule of the law which, simply put, says, "everything is wearing out." Any form of human "progress" means interference with these cycles and their balances. Ecology can help us keep the problems down, but getting rid of them will probably be impossible. This is the price tag of man's civilization. It is good to remember that environmentalists drive cars and use products that create pollution. The shoe of guilt fits just as well on the foot of non-Christians as on Christians. We're all caught in the problems together.

See also "Design"

38

IS A WORLDWIDE FLOOD POSSIBLE?

Does modern science rule out a worldwide flood? While not everyone agrees that there was such a flood, not everyone agrees that it would be impossible, either.

It is not unscientific for us to look at this. Most of the world's peoples have a tradition of a worldwide flood which destroyed everything. But one family and the animals which they had taken with them in some sort of a boat were saved.   Many scientists have believed this, too.

There are many geological and fossil evidences which are better-explained by a worldwide flood. Many of these evidences *cannot* be explained by uniformitarianism.

Of course science can only study the evidences of Noah's flood which remain on the earth. But the Bible remains our most certain and complete record of the flood because it is from God.

The World Before the Flood

Evolutionists and creationists both believe that the early earth was a much warmer place than it is now. This is why we find the remains of tropical plants and animals in polar regions of the earth today. Creationists have said that this may be because there was a canopy of water vapor in the atmosphere of the earth. Such a canopy would act like the roof of a greenhouse, capturing and holding the heating rays of the sun.

The canopy would have made the earth warmer and more humid. But it would not have blocked out the sun or the stars.

A vapor canopy is scientifically possible. Some scientists have said that this is what Venus has—except that the vapor is not mostly water vapor. Joseph Dillow, a scientist who has studied the atmosphere of earth, says that it would have been possible for the earth to have had such a canopy. There would be nothing supernatural about the earth having such a canopy. He has shown that the earth would have been warm and tropical with such a canopy. Present life could live very well in these conditions.

Genesis 1:6-8 talks about God separating the waters from the waters. Many creation scienists believe that this may be a reference to such a water canopy.

Dillow also says that volcanoes threw dust into the air. This dust collected the water droplets of the vapor canopy, and caused them to fall as rain.

Dillow has put together a detailed scientific picture of the events to see if this would work. He has computed the amount of dust which would be needed to turn the canopy into falling rain. He found that the 1912 eruption of the volcano Katmai, for example, would have provided more than enough dust to cause the entire canopy to turn to rain. And the 1912 eruption of Katmai did not even produce the huge amount of dust which Mount Tambora did in 1815!

Dillow says that many volcanoes all over the world erupted to bring about the collapse of the canopy into rain. Dillow thinks that the water fall from the canopy would have been equal to four inches per hour or more, on a non-stop basis.

MT. ST. HELEN'S FROM THE GROUND AS IT BLOWS STEAM AND ASH INTO THE SKY.

This water would have fallen from the sky producing hurricane-like conditions all over the world. It could have lasted for over a month. This water falling from the sky would have mixed with the waters gushing from the ground. In this amount of time the earth could have been entirely covered with water.

If the vapor canopy had not collapsed at Noah's time, the volcanic eruptions which have taken place often since that time could have caused the same Flood—even in our own day. This knowledge adds new meaning to God's promise never to bring such a flood upon the earth again!

Evidences of Catastrophism

If such a worldwide flood took place, we should certainly be able to find evidences of such great violence in the rocks of the earth.

Uniformitarian geologists say that the rocks are very old. By observing present-day rates at which silt settles in water, they estimate that only one foot of sediment is deposited every 2 to 5 thousand years. So, a rock layer 10 feet thick would need 20,000 years to form, according what they say.

The fact that fossils exist calls this into question. Any dead creature which has to wait around for hundreds or thousands of years before it is covered and protected from decay will never become a fossil. The fact that there are millions of fossils says that this rate of sediment deposit is violated very often.

Shell fish fossils are plentiful. Yet if even the shells are exposed for very long after death, they begin to dissolve and erode. The uniformist rate of settling would take 1,000 years to bury a shell only five inches in diameter. Many fossil clams are found in the closed position. When clams die under quiet conditions, they are open. But when they are disturbed, they close up. When they are found in the closed position, encased in rock, as many if not most are, they are closed. This means they were disturbed and buried in sediment while they were still alive.

We do not need these evidences of the flood to prove that the Bible is true. Faith convinces us that the Bible is true in every word, whether it is talking about our salvation or the physical history of the world.

Ripple marks on the beach normally do not last more than a few hours before they are worn away by wind or water. Fossil ripple marks are often found on the upper surface of rock layers. This means that they were covered before they had time to erode.

Fossil Graveyards

When a fish dies it decays very quickly. Experimenters from Chicago's Museum of Natural History found that a dead fish which was not disturbed by other creatures would not only completely decay in six days, but even the skeleton would completely come apart. But in Scotland there is a ten-thousand-square-mile area which is packed very tightly with billions of fish. They were buried alive by tons of earth. What could have collected billions of fish together like this and then buried them over a ten-thousand-square-mile area?

Every continent in the world also has at least one dinosaur graveyard containing millions of dinosaurs which were buried all together—intermixed with each other! A dinosaur fossil graveyard in Belgium has dinosuars buried in stacks over 100 feet thick.

Creation scientists ask, could the vast beds of sedimentary strata which we find covering three-quarters of the earth's surface, with their buried remains of life, result from the infinitely slow processes we see today?

The answer is certainly **NO!** These fossil beds were created when the raging flood waters fell from the sky and gushed forth in oceans from the depths of the earth, just as Scripture records. These waters swept up all in their path and deposited them together.

See also "Fossil Record," "Coal," and "Petroleum"

FOSSIL FACTS — WHAT FOSSILS ARE

In almost any discussion of creation and evolution, sooner or later the question comes up, "What about the fossils?" It is often asked by sincere young people who are confused about the difference between what they are taught in school and the view of life the Bible presents. Sometimes Christian parents and church leaders are stumped by questions like: "What about the dinosaurs?" and "Why was the 'prehistoric' world so different from today's?" or "Why do the rocks lie to us?".

Such questions also show how much success evolutionists have had in bringing people to think about the world in their way. Young people who are looking for the truth have a right to be confused. Do you know what fossils are?

Some people have come to think that just the *existence* of the fossils by themselves is strong evidence for evolution. This is because they have been taught this in school and have been so influenced by popular media presentations. What we will find may surprise you. Not only is evolution not well supported by the fossils, it is even contradicted by them. And even more surprisingly to some, the Biblical-creationist view of life is better supported by the fossils.

So how did things get so turned around? Why do so many people (especially scientists) believe in evolution if the fossils do not prove it? Are evolutionists lying to people, or trying to fool them? We will talk about this question in our next article. Just now, we need to start at the beginning, which is with the fossils themselves.

What are fossils? Fossils are the preserved remains of animals or plants that once were alive. Most of the time they are found in sedimentary (water-laid) rocks that were once soft muds and slurries, like cement. Over time, the muds hardened into stone. Some fossils are also found in volcanic rock, and a few are found in things like ice, tar and amber (hardened tree sap). In the case of animals, generally the soft parts such as flesh, hide and hair have decayed and only the skeleton remains in the rock, but the soft parts sometime make *prints* in the rock. It is hard to tell exactly what an animal looked like from its fossil skeleton, but you can sometimes get some ideas about what the animal *might* have looked like. You need to remember that pictures of dinosaurs in books are only artists' ideas. Their colors, shapes and body coverings are all missing and had to be imagined. The same thing is true of so-called "ape-men" often seen in the same books. They are the result of evolutionists' imaginations and artists' drawings.

Many plants are also preserved as fossils, and often the details of their appearance are clearer than with animals. In some cases, the plant's material has been replaced by minerals, and it is said to be *petrified* (turne to stone).

Fossils are found in sedimentary rock layers all over the world, except for a very few places. The total depth of all these layers is usually between one and about three miles. This is a *lot* of water-laid material, and it has great numbers of animals and plants of every type. Some of these are now *extinct* (no longer living).

Fossil animals are often found in large beds. The remains of many different types, both predator and prey, are found together with their bones mixed and not scavenged (eaten on). The Karoo formation in South Africa is estimated to contain the remains of 800,000 MILLION animals! This is a lot of dead animals, and the question comes up, Why would they all get together at one time for a great dying-out party? It seems very clear that only rising water could herd all these different animals together into one place and then drown and bury them.

THIS IS A PHOTO OF A TRILOBITE IN CRETACEOUS LIMESTONE. ACCORDING TO EVOLUTION THIS TRILOBITE IS AN INDEX FOSSIL WHICH DIED OUT SOME 230 MILLION YEARS AGO *OVER 100 MILLION YEARS EARLIER THAN EVOLUTIONARY DATES GIVEN FOR THIS CRETACEOUS LIMESTONE!* THESE FOSSILS HELP SHOW THAT THE EVOLUTIONARY IDEA IS NOT BASED ON FACT. (*This trilobite is from the Sommervel County Museum (Glen Rose, Texas) with the kind permission of Museum Director, Jean Mack. Photo: William Overn.*)

It is important that burial take place soon after death if a fossil is to form. In the world today, very few fossils are formed because when an animal dies, it is usually eaten by other animals, or it decays. Nowhere today are fossils being formed on the scale that we find them in the rocks because it takes a great catastrophe to kill and bury thousands or millions of animals. In a *worldwide* flood, there would be no escape. Keep that in mind when evolutionists talk about small floods.

Keep this one point in mind. The fossils by themselves do not tell us very much. They are simply *there*. Something happened to form them, but they do not come with dates on them or with death certificates. Men must MAKE UP A STORY or ACCEPT A STORY GIVEN TO THEM to explain what happened.

The made-up story is evolution. The story given to us is the Bible's. It is as simple as that. And the Bible's story fits the facts best with the fewest contradictions and problems.

This is the general order of fossils as they tend to be found in the rocks, from bottom (earliest) to top (latest). The simpler, usually marine-type animals tend to be in the deeper layers, while the more complex and intelligent animals tend to be in the upper layers.

This general order to the fossils is one of the main evidences for evolution. The simpler animals are supposed to have evolved first, and so would be in the earliest rocks. The more complex animals evolved later and would be in the uppermost rocks. That is what we would expect if evolution were true. Very often it is this way, BUT this is not a *proof* of evolution. If evolution really happened, we would not expect to find any exceptions to this order. But as we shall see, there are many exceptions to this order.

The rule should be "oldest rocks are lower." But as we shall see, this is not really the way it is done. It may often be the case, but we should expect it *always* to be true, unless the earth has played some trick to get the rock layers reversed. Most people do not know how rocks are dated. They are *not* dated by their position relative to other rocks and not by what they are made of. They are dated by looking at them to see if they contain certain kinds of fossils that were dominant during certain periods that we just named. These are called *index fossils*. When a certain index fossil is present, then an age is given to the rock containing it. This is all done by first arranging the fossils and then *guessing* (what else?) about how long it must have taken to evolve into something else. How long does it take to turn a lizard into a bird? If you are getting the idea that this is a lot of guessing, you are right. And it is even worse than that.

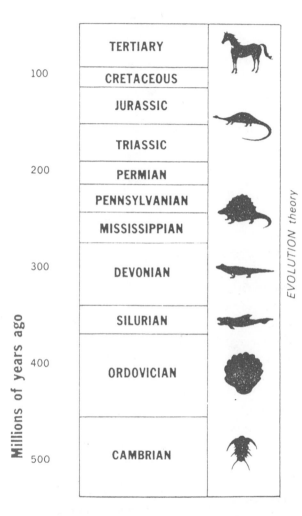

Millions of years ago		
100	TERTIARY	
	CRETACEOUS	
	JURASSIC	
	TRIASSIC	
200	PERMIAN	
	PENNSYLVANIAN	
	MISSISSIPPIAN	
300	DEVONIAN	
	SILURIAN	
400	ORDOVICIAN	
500	CAMBRIAN	

EVOLUTION theory

HOW A FOSSIL IS MADE

Buried quickly

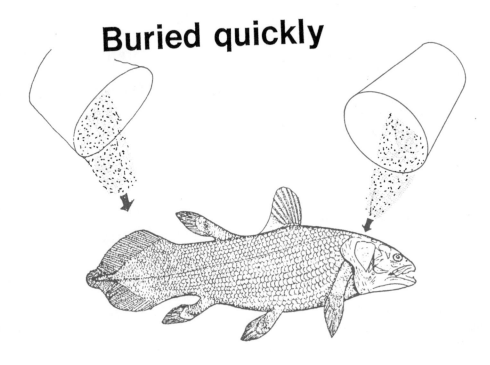

There is a system of reasoning in a circle here. The rocks are dated by the fossils. But this can only be right if evolution is really true. This is one reason we call evolution a faith. If you ask a paleontologist (a scientist who studies fossils) "How do you know your fossils are old?", he will answer, "Because the simpler fossils are found in the oldest rocks." If you then go to a geologist and ask him "How do you know which rocks are oldest?", he will say, "The oldest rocks have the simplest fossils." Really! That is a kind of mental "ring-around-the-rosie" called "circular reasoning." You cannot use something (evolution theory) to prove itself to be true. But this is what is actually done.

At the same time, since the Bible says that all of the different kinds of plants and animals were created fully formed, and because it says that they all reproduce "after their kind," we would not expect to find any "transitional forms." In light of the Bible we would *expect* to find just what we *do* find.

Next, we notice that many fossil deposits are HUGE. We mentioned the Karoo formation earlier. There are no fossil-forming actions going on in the world today that compare to what is found in the rocks. Dead animals today are generally eaten or decay before they can be fossilized. Catastrophes today are tiny (compared to what is in the rocks), and animals tend to escape many of

The idea of a worldwide flood is further strengthened by the rock formations themselves. Many of them are HUGE and THICK — vast areas of the American southwest are covered by beds of red sandstone up to 2,000 feet thick. And these layers are nearly uniform in composition. What kind of river flood could lay down a formation of such size? Nothing like it is seen in modern times.

The case with fossil plants is even worse.

There are both animals and plants that are sandwiched in between several layers of sedimentary rock. In coal seams and other places, fossil tree trunks often extend 30-40 feet through several layers of sediment. Shall we believe that these trees grew there, died, somehow remained anchored at the bottom and withstood millions of years of weather without rotting or falling down, while these layers of rock built up around them? That's ridiculous! It is obvious that the trees were washed in and covered over with mud and sediments very rapidly before they could decay. It is worth noticing that there is no evidence of weathering or erosion at the edges of the rock layers. This witnesses to their being deposited rapidly.

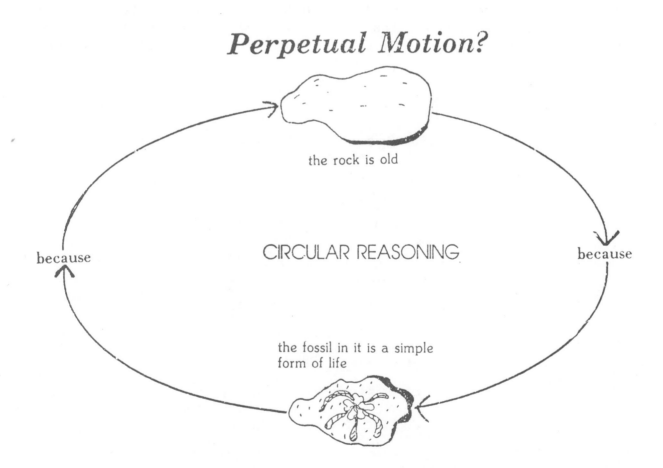

Perpetual Motion?

the rock is old

CIRCULAR REASONING

because

because

the fossil in it is a simple form of life

them. What does this tell us? Just that the disaster that killed the animals in the rocks did not offer them any chance of escape. It seems very simple and logical that only a great, worldwide flood would herd so many animals of all kinds together in various places and then drown and bury them together. There would be no escape. There would be no other animals around to eat the dead or scavenge the bones. In a great flood the bones would be mixed together — which is the way they are found. It does not seem reasonable that small, local floods could make the great fossil graveyards of the world.

Another immense problem is that of rock layers that are out of place. We mean out of place in *their* system. We saw before that the oldest rocks should always be lower, with younger ones on top. But there are large areas where this order is *reversed*. In Glacier Park, Montana, a very large (about 12,000 miles) thick (about three miles) block of Precambrian limestone (very old) is sitting directly atop a

mass of Cretaceous (dinosaur-age) shale. How did it get there? If the rocks were laid down in that order, the evolutionary rock-dating system is all wrong. So, say evolutionists, the rocks must have moved or been moved. The older layers were folded upward and then shoved sideways, coming to rest on top of the younger rocks. This is the "overthrust" explanation. There is only one problem. There is NO evidence of movement of the rock mass, and when rocks move, they leave marks. So we are faced with either a great miracle or a great mistake.

This situation of reversed order rocks is common. There are several other sizeable "overthrusts" in the American West and some in Europe. Sometimes just certain layers belonging to certain Periods are missing. The Grand Canyon, for example, one of the best exposures of layers in the world, is missing Ordovician, Silurian, most of the Devonian Periods and all the Pennsylvanian — about *100 million years of rock strata are gone with-*

THIS CORYTHOSAURUS, OR HELMETED DINOSAUR, IS MORE COMMONLY KNOWN AS THE DUCK-BILL DINOSAUR. THIS SKELETON, MADE FROM FOSSILIZED BONES OF THE CREATURE FOUND IN ALBERTA, CANADA IS 18 FEET TALL AND 33 FEET LONG. (*Courtesy of the Natural History Museum of Philadelphia.*)

out a trace! All this should tell us that something is very wrong with evolutionary geology. Evolutionists excuse the missing strata by saying erosion removed them, but there is no evidence of this. In fact, the absence of erosion between strata boundaries is an evidence of their being rapidly deposited by a flood.

The creation explanation for most of the fossils is very simple. We believe the great Flood of Noah's day, as recorded in the Bible, is responsible for most of the earth's sedimentary rocks and the animals and plants buried in them. The more you study the evidence, the more convincing it becomes. A worldwide flood would have the range and power to form the huge geological deposits. It would herd many types of animals together in different places and drown and bury them together. It would bury and compress plants and animals to form coal and oil rapidly. It would change the entire face of the earth, and that is what we believe it did.

Creationists do not have any problems with out-of-order rock layers. A worldwide flood could have laid down any type of rock in any order, containing all sorts of fossils. We cannot pin down its actions exactly, of course. Moving water is complex and does tricky things. No humans were there (except Noah and his family and they didn't take any pictures). We have to take God's Word about the Flood. But it is interesting that almost every culture on earth has a flood story. These myths sometimes are strikingly close to the Bible's account. Aborigines living in the Australian desert have a flood story. Why would that be? — unless their ancestors passed the real story down to them over the centuries. Over the years the details might be repeated differently, but the main theme is clear. The world was destroyed by a great flood early in man's history.

It is too bad modern geologists reject the idea of Noah's Flood as the cause of the world's fossils. It would be the golden key that would unlock many of the earth's puzzling features, which evolution cannot explain. But modern science has mostly been taken over by the faith of evolution, and what we get for explanations are clever excuses. But the evidence is there, it is real and it won't go away. It is only a matter of time before evolution, like many fossils, will be crushed by the weight of the evidence.

Every Christian has an obligation to not only study the Bible, but to study other works that help make the Bible's message clear and understandable. We hope you will make a careful study of creationism so you can defend your faith and give good, convincing answers to those who want to know what you believe and why. The Bible commands you to do this (I Peter 3:15). It is a big responsibility to understand the truth about the origin of this world, and an incredible privilege to know the Lord Who personally created it.

Collect some pictures of fossil animals and plants and note how they are like the types still living, if the line is not extinct.

You might write United States Geological Survey asking for free information on the geology (evolutionary, of course) of their area. You can then try to reinterpret it in terms of flood geology. This might also give you information on the best areas for field trips and personal fossil hunting.

See also "Flood"

49

Fossil Man

More has been written on human fossils than on any other kind of fossils. Book after book on the library shelf is filled with beautifully painted, full-color pictures of early people and apemen. All of this makes these "ape-men" more real to us. Pictures often say more than the real scientific evidence does.

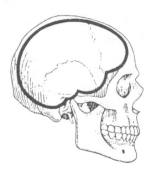

MAN

You might be surprised to learn that we really have very few human fossils. There are no complete skeletons. For most "early man" fossils we have at most a few bone pieces, maybe a bit of skull and a few teeth. Heidelberg man, for example, is known by but a single piece of a jawbone.

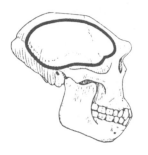

HOMO ERECTUS

Nor can we draw a complete picture of a creature through fossils. Even a complete fossil does not preserve soft parts such as lips, hair, nose, eyebrows, facial expression, ears, or muscles. Think how your own skull would appear if stripped of your hair and face, and covered instead with fur! When we see pictures of early man we must remember how much of the artist's imagination is involved. One supposed "early man," *Zinjanthropus*, for example, was fleshed out in very different ways. One way he looked just like an ape. Another way he looked just like us. Which way was right?

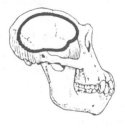

CHIMPANZEE

The Bible tells us that the first human being looked pretty much the way we do. God made apes separately from people.

If a scientist believes that evolution is true, he will try to make the bones he has found fit into evolution. If a scientist believes that man was created by God in his present form, he will know that any human-like bones are either all-man, or all-ape, (or even all-something else.)

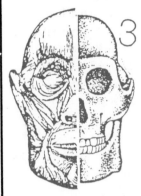

DEEP-MUSCLE ADDITION

Next, the molding artist uses more clay to form the deep muscles which were attached to the original bone. Muscle markings on any original bone help show where these muscles were.

RECONSTRUCTIONS

STEPS IN RECONSTRUCTING A FOSSIL HEAD

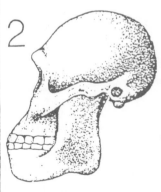

ORIGINAL FRAGMENT

The reconstruction of a fossil head is a jigsaw puzzle. It begins by deciding what part of the head the parts of bone belonged to, and then putting them together. (Reconstructions are regularly done starting with even less bone than shown here.)

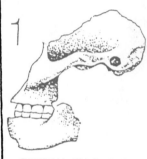

RECONSTRUCTED SKULL

In the first stage of reconstruction the molder adds clay to the original piece of bone to make a complete bone. The smaller the original piece, the less accurate the reconstruction is.

4

FINISHED HEAD

After the clay for the fatty tissue has been added to the tip of the nose, chin and ears, a skin covering is applied. Details such as skin color, and hair can only be guessed at.

IN THE CASE OF "LUCY" THE ENTIRE SKULL WAS RECONSTRUCTED FROM A FAIRLY FLAT PIECE OF BONE THE SIZE OF YOUR THUMBNAIL!

WHO WERE THE CAVEMEN?

What were people really like many years ago? If you have watched Old West programs on television, you get the idea that people in the 1800's were pretty much like people today. But what if you go back to very ancient history? Were people a long time ago like people today?

Ugh! Grunt! Bam!

We all have cartoon-like images in our minds of cavemen. But creation scientists say man was created fully human from the beginning.

There really is no such thing as a time which is not covered by historical records. Scripture begins with the beginning of creation. Since this history was written by God, we can trust it completely.

Known Scientific Explanations

It turns out that the cavemen were not really brutes. Consider Neanderthal man. When he was first discovered, scientists noticed marks on the bones which seemed to show that Neanderthal had very big strong neck muscles. Why did Neanderthal man need such strong muscles? They thought that Neanderthal must have had a stooped posture with his head pushed forward — a sure sign that he evolved from the apes.

But later examination by evolutionary scientists led them to admit that the shape of the skeletons of many fossil Neanderthals were from poor diet and bad climate. The first Neanderthals discovered lived in harsh climates where diseases like rickets and arthritis were common.

Neanderthal man, in fact, walked as striaght as the rest of us. One newspaper editorial at the time ran the headline: "Neanderthal Man Straightens Up!" Books had to be rewritten and museums had to make their Neanderthal models stand up. Today Neanderthal man is classified as fully human.

Recent articles have even pointed out that if you dressed Neanderthal in a business suit and let him walk down any city street he would not even attract any attention. Neanderthal has gone from brute to business suit!

The Problem with Lack of Information

Changes of mind, such as the changing view of Neanderthal, are common in the study of human "evolution." In no other field of science do opinions differ so greatly. Each scientist working in human evolution has a different theory of man's family tree. In no other field can one have fame so quickly for making an "important" find. This has often led to claims for new discoveries being made before all the facts were in. Sometimes it has even led to admitted frauds:

Nebraska man — was reconstructed from a single tooth which turned out to be the tooth of an extinct wild pig.

Java man — whose discoverer hid the fossils from the public for 30 years, and then revealed that he had found fully human fossils in the same rock layer.

Zinjanthropus — whose discoverer, Louis Leakey, received great publicity for his find and later admitted that it was simply another *Australopithecus.*

Piltdown man — who was a deliberate hoax.

The biggest problem is that there are

few bones to work with. Even many of these bones are not complete. Reconstructions can only be made using educated guesses about what the muscles looked like and where they were. How much hair there was, and where that hair belongs, as well as skin color have to be total guesses.

There are a lot of other interesting fossil-related items we can only mention briefly. Many fossil animals appear too early or too late in the rocks. A lot of evolutionary dates have had to be reset or shuffled around. Some types of fossil animals thought extinct are still alive; the Coelecanth fish is an example. And it is *unchanged* over a supposed 60-million-year span of time! What does that tell us?

Human skulls and whole skeletons have been found in rocks too early for them, but evolutionists excuse them as burials, even though some do not look that way. And there are artifacts and footprints where they do not belong. An iron pot was found in a lump of coal,[6] and a nice little hammer[7] made of iron with a wood handle has been found in Silurian (3rd Period) sandstone — far too early for human tools to appear. And of course, there are the famous Paluxy River footprints.

In the riverbed of the Paluxy River in Texas are dinosaur and human footprints *together*. They are well investigated and documented, and appear human and genuine. But evolutionists will generally not even go down to investigate them. We know why, don't we? If they are real, it is all over for evolution.

 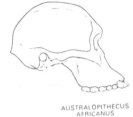

AUSTRALOPITHECUS AFRICANUS

The Christian who believes that man was hand-made by God in pretty much his present form should know that there is no scientific evidence for human evolution. Because of what Scripture says, we may be sure that no evidence which supports human evolution will ever be found.

For many years, evolutionists have been arguing over man's supposed ancestry from the monkeys, apes or ape-like somethings they have been digging up. But their picture of man's ancestors has gotten more confusing over time, instead of clearer. For instance: Piltdown Man was a hoax, a joke. Nebraska Man was just a pig's tooth. Java Man is a suspected fraud, believed to be a giant gibbon. Neanderthal Man was supposed to be a hulking, stooped-over, hairy, apish brute, until scientists found out his skeleton showed signs of arthritis and was deformed. Further study has shown Neanderthals were a fully human race. Then came the Australopithecines (means "Southern Ape"). There has been controversy over whether they should be considered ancestral to man or not. Then Richard Leakey in the early '70's discovered a modern-type skull in strata that was dated older than that of the Australopithecines! The skull was called "1470" after its museum number. It caused a lot of debate because man can't be older than his ancestors! The arguments go on and on, but the picture doesn't get any clearer. Man has always been man, since God made him that way.

See also "Anthropology"

THE GALAPAGOS ISLANDS — AN ISOLATED WORLD

Isolated ocean islands are a biologist's paradise. Since they are located far from continental shores, the forms of life on them are often odd and unusual. The only plants and animals on them are those that have drifted, swum, or flown to their shores, and once there, the new populations are subject to inbreeding and a fairly even environment. So, the assortment of life forms and relationships to each other tends to be special.

Since animals and plants in such a situation may be without their natural enemies, they may build a large population of just a few types very quickly. And there is less competition for "living space." So plants or animals may choose a way of living that they might not in a normal situation.

Such a situation can be found on a group of oceanic islands called the Galapagos (Gul-LAH-puh-gus) Islands. Charles Robert Darwin, although he had no formal scientific training, had shipped on board a British exploration ship, the *Beagle*, as a naturalist. It was largely his observations of the animals of the Galapagos that "jelled" the theory of evolution in his mind, and caused him to become convinced of its truth. The later impact on the scientific world was great. So we who believe in God's creating work need to pay attention to these islands and what Darwin found on them.

The Galapagos are desolate, rocky, volcanic islands rising 10,000 feet from the Pacific ocean floor. They are located some 600 miles west of Ecuador, sitting on the equator. The chain of islands is made up of 14 islands, with an area of 2869 square miles. The largest island is 75 miles long.

There are no springs or fresh water sources on the islands, since the volcanic rock is too porous to trap rainfall. It doesn't rain there very often either. Sometimes it rains only once about every four years. This might seem odd for islands on the equator, but the cold-water Humboldt current comes up the coast of South America and swings westward out to sea at the Galapagos. Only when a warm current mixes with it does rain come. The cold water allows penguins and sea lions to live there, despite the mild weather.

Another unusual animal on the Galapagos is the marine iguana. These lizards feed in the sea. They have long, curved toenails and short, strong legs so they can cling to rocks as waves wash over them. Their tail is flattened sideways, so it can be used as an oar to propel their body through the water. Their teeth are especially made for grazing on algae. And this lizard can do something other reptiles cannot. It can dive down to the bottom in 70-degree water, which is 25 degrees colder than the land, and eat algae. This would slow down any other reptile so much it couldn't move. The Galapagos are truly full of animal surprises.

Land iguanas are the cousins of the marine iguanas. They are found nowhere else but the Galapagos. They feed on tree-sized cactus plants, eating pads, flowers, fruits, spines and all. They have no natural enemies and grow to a much larger size than their ancestors on the mainland.

Because of the unusual features of the Galapagos animals, evolutionists like to consider them to be clear examples of evolution. But one simple fact speaks loud and clear. For all the special differences, the tortoises are still tortoises, and the iguanas are still iguanas, and they are still like the mainland forms from which they are descended. There is no evidence of transformation of one kind of animal into a different kind, and this is what evolution requires.

This Marine Iguana was warming himself on the rocks on Hood Island. Note the long claws. *(Photo: Walter Lang.)*

Turtles are supposed to have been around for 175 million years, longer than the dinosaurs. Why would the whole race of dinosaurs vanish, and the turtle be the survivor? You can hardly say that the turtle is smarter, stronger, faster, or better adapted for anything, except that its shell gives it good protection. Evolution has no answer for why the dinosaurs disappeared and turtles survived, or why fossil turtles look so much like today's turtles, or where the turtles' ancestors are. The answer

Darwin's famous finches are very often put forward as a good example of evolution. Let's learn about them. What is a finch? It's a small-to-medium-sized bird, a member of the seedeater family, which is the largest of the bird families. About 1/7 of all birds are seed-eaters. They are found all over the world except in Australia. Some sing well, and some are very pretty colored, such as the cardinal, the grosbeaks, and the painted bunting. They all have short, strong, cone-shaped beaks designed for seed-cracking. The scientific name of the family is *Fringillidae*.

Darwin studied various groups of finches and discovered that they differed from each other in certain ways, such as beak size, total body size, plumage details, and life-styles. Some ate insects, some ate large seeds, some ate small seeds. Some ate fruit, some ate cacti, and one even became sort of a woodpecker. The Woodpecker Finch uses a cactus spine to dig insects out of tree bark like a woodpecker uses its tongue! This is one of the very few examples of tool-using animals, and perhaps is the only tool-using bird. How the bird got this habit is unknown. Perhaps birds are smarter than we thought. It apparently *learned* this trick, since it is not an instinct with finches. There is much yet to be learned about all God's creatures.

THE TRAIL OF A TORTOISE THROUGH THE SAND ON FLOREANA ISLAND. *(Photo: Walter Lang.)*

from the Galapagos is that there is such a thing as VARIATION, and a good deal of it, but no large-scale evolution is possible.

There are ground-dwelling, bush-dwelling, and tree-dwelling finches. BUT THEY ARE ALL FINCHES. Darwin looked at all this variety and knew that it had to develop from one or several pairs of birds that had come from

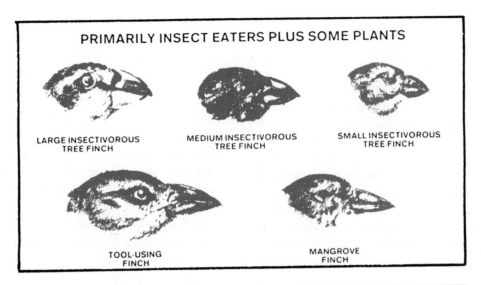

PRIMARILY INSECT EATERS PLUS SOME PLANTS

LARGE INSECTIVOROUS TREE FINCH

MEDIUM INSECTIVOROUS TREE FINCH

SMALL INSECTIVOROUS TREE FINCH

TOOL-USING FINCH

MANGROVE FINCH

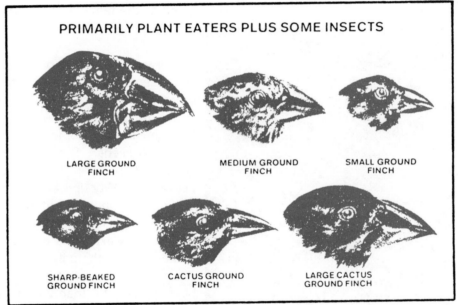

PRIMARILY PLANT EATERS PLUS SOME INSECTS

LARGE GROUND FINCH

MEDIUM GROUND FINCH

SMALL GROUND FINCH

SHARP-BEAKED GROUND FINCH

CACTUS GROUND FINCH

LARGE CACTUS GROUND FINCH

the mainland. Since the islands were wide open for life forms, with little or no competition, the finches could select different places to live and styles of life, depending on how much competition for food developed in an area. Evolutionists like to point to this as evolution; creationists would call it ''adaptive variation.'' The point to see is that the finches, try as they might, were unable to become anything other than finches. The woodpecker finch has to use a tool because HE WAS UNABLE TO EVOLVE THE RIGHT KIND OF BEAK AND TONGUE, like the woodpecker has. It seems incredible that Darwin would miss this point, but he did. He looked at all this finch variety and drew a very different conclusion.

Creationists who have studied Darwin's finches all agree that the birds show only minor differences. These really should not be called evolution. No new basic types of bird have appeared. The changes that can be seen include bill shape, body size, skull features, and differences in feathers. But all of the birds are still very much finches. All these variations could be produced by breeders in a few years, something that Darwin knew quite well. Some people call such changes "microevolution." But creationists feel this is a bad word, since it leads people to think that major changes in form (macroevolution) must be possible. But there is not a shred of evidence for this.

Darwin sorted his finches out into thirteen different species. Because they all had come from one or a few pairs, he decided evolution had taken place. But scientists do not agree on just what defines a species. Creationists do not think of species today as the same as a created "kind" as described in the Bible. But in Darwin's day, this was what church authorities were teaching. We will see in our next article all the trouble this caused.

So despite the strange arrangements, lifestyles, and unusual features of the Galapagos animals, we would have to conclude that these come from genetic ability for variation that God had built into them. Plants and animals need to have some flexibility to adjust and adapt in special ways to a fairly wide range of conditions if they are to survive over wide areas in the world. In His care for all creatures God would have done this. He knew, when He created them, that after the Flood He would send them all over the world and they would have to live in different conditions than they were used to. But this ability to change and adjust is limited, and this is the heart of Darwin's great mistake about the Galapagos.

It seems strange that Darwin, who was an intelligent man, should have missed the fact that no evidence of large-scale evolution was to be found on the Galapagos. Perhaps he *wanted* evolution to be true so much that he overlooked this obvious piece of evidence. And then he could have had help in making his mistake: II Corinthians 4:4 says, "In whom the god of this world (Satan) hath blinded the minds of them which believe not, lest the light of the glorious gospel of Christ, who is the image of God, should shine unto them."

What we see from this verse is that the Devil helps people make mistakes, if their faith is not in God. What this shows is that this matter of creation and evolution is not just a clash of opposing philosophies of men. It is a conflict of spirits as well, that of God, and his enemy, Satan. This is the real reason for the importance of this debate.

Creationists today would say that Darwin's findings on the Galapagos are simply not an issue. There is no problem. But we would deny that either the Galapagos or Darwin's finches prove evolution. Finches can change only so much. Their limits are coded into their genes. We would have to say that Darwin's great leap of faith in believing in the idea of large-scale evolution was a mistake. And a serious one at that, which we are trying to correct and keep others from making.

See also "Design"

59

Giraffe

Giraffes and Headaches

The long neck of the giraffe presents a special problem in the design of living things. How do you keep the blood pressure around a place like the brain at safe levels when that brain is on the end of the neck of a giraffe which can swing from ground level to dozens of feet above the ground?

To begin with, the giraffe heart is probably the most powerful in the animal kingdom. It takes about double normal pressure to pump blood up that long neck to the brain. In addition, the giraffe spreads his front legs apart when he stoops to drink. This lowers the level of the heart and reduces the difference in height from the heart to the head of the drinking animal. But more than this is needed. So there are valves in the neck veins. These close when the head is lower to keep blood from flowing back down into the brain.

But all of this is still not enough to take care of the problems. So the giraffe has something called the wonder net. This is a spongy tissue filled with lots of small blood vessels. It is near the base of the brain. The blood first flows through this net of vessels before it reaches the brain. It is believed that the spinal fluid, which bathes the brain and spinal column, also produces a pressure which prevents the breaking of the brain's blood vessels. In order to support all of this, the walls of the giraffe's arteries are thicker than in any other mammal.

If the giraffe evolved it had to be without trial and error. There would have been no room for mistake. Darwin said that the long neck was the result of reaching for higher food and thus the giraffe survived when other animals with shorter necks did not. But Darwin had no answer as to why there were these check valves and spongy wonder nets in the giraffe, and not in other animals.

Did you ever see how God has filled the creation with the evidence that He created? Knowledge in itself does not lead away from God. People begin to believe in things like evolution when they want to give up God and explain things without Him.

Horse Sense About the Horse Series

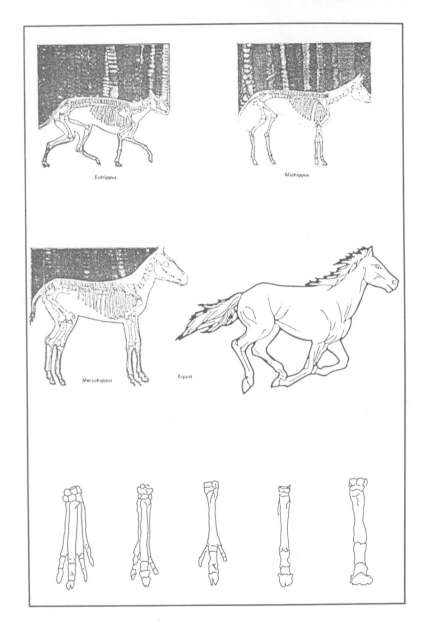

Eohippus

Miohippus

Merychippus

Equus

The famous ''horse series'' of fossils is supposed to prove evolution beyond a doubt. It appears in nearly every textbook on evolution, and in countless museum displays. What you see is a series of skeletons, starting with an animal about the size of a fox, which gets progressively larger with successive forms, and ends with a modern horse skeleton. It begins as a four-toed animal, apparently becoming three-toed, and then ends as a one-toed (hoofed) horse. There are similarities in the head skeletons in all of them. It almost seems that all these forms are laid out just like that out in the field, and you could dig them up in just that order. We will see about that.

Here are the scientific names given to the animals in this series: 1-*Eohippus*, 2-*Orohippus*, 3-*Opihippus*, 4-*Mesohippus*, 5-*Miohip-*

61

pus, 6-*Parahippus*, 7-*Merychippus*, 8-*Protohippus*, *Pliohippus*, *Hipparion* (friends), 9-*Plesippus*, 10-*Equus*. The "hippus" ending is Greek for horse. Eohippus means "dawn horse" and the last form, *Equus*, is the Latin word for horse.

Another odd thing. The number of ribs on different forms of "horses" keeps switching around. Get this: *Eohippus* had 18 pairs of ribs. *Orehippus* had only 15 pairs. *Pliohippus* jumped to 19 pairs, and *Equus Scotti* is back to 18. What's going on? Can't evolution decide how many ribs a horse ought to have? This should make us very suspicious about the truth of the whole thing. And there are sudden jumps in size between forms, as well as the toe changes, BUT NO SLOW TRANSITIONS BETWEEN THEM. It begins to look like what we have here is a well-arranged stack of animal skeletons that look similar, but may have been entirely different animals, with different habits. They may have lived at the same time, but were differently buried. Scientists have done the sorting and arranging. This is called STACKING THE DECK.

Creationist Frank Cousins says that the family tree of the horse is neat and continuous only in textbooks. Scientific philosopher Norman Macbeth claims scientists practice a double standard, one for the public and one for professional scientists. This is simply to say that the textbooks and displays are misleading and dishonest. Macbeth wrote an evolutionist author about this; the author replied that such over-simplification of the facts is alright because the audience doesn't know much science. In other words, only the professionals get to know the truth. Mr. Macbeth protested this as "improper and unwise."

Eohippus may not have been a horse at all. Its skeleton is nearly identical to an animal living today, the daman, or Hyrax. The type of teeth of *Eohippus* were browsing-type teeth. These are for eating leaves off bushes. Somewhere, somehow, there was a changeover to grazing-type teeth which the modern horse has; these are for eating grass. Grass has a lot of sand in it, and special teeth are needed for handling it. Also, the animal's digestive system would have to be changed to fit the switch. When and how did all this happen? Does anybody know? Why are they keeping it a secret?

**Evolution and Creation —
Historical Models**

QUICK DICTIONARY

MACROEVOLUTION: Large-scale change in living things, like a change from a fish to an amphibian. (Has never been *seen*).

MICROEVOLUTION: Small-scale change in the appearance of living things without making anything *new*, such as in the breeding of dogs.

ADAPTATION: Often preferred over **MICROEVOLUTION** by creation scientists since no new things have been formed in the living thing. When this term is used by an evolutionist, it may be used to suggest that new things have evolved.

The debate between evolutionary scientists and creation scientists is a debate about the nature of biological change. We can see that living things change. Both evolutionists and creationists accept the same facts and the same present theories about them. Both accept the normal variation that we see in breeding experiments.

But creation scientists and evolutionary scientists don't agree on what to *call* this minor variation. Evolutionists believe it is part of the process that leads to new kinds of animals. So they call it "evolution." Creationists believe there is good evidence that small-scale changes *don't* lead to new animals. They prefer not to call it "evolution." Creation scientists use two different terms here. They use the term *micro* to refer to small changes. They use *macro*, as in *macro*evolution, to refer to changes of one animal into another.

The Difference Makes a Difference

Where evolutionists and creationists part company is not in their modern scientific theories but in their historical models. Evolutionists believe that animals can change in almost unlimited ways. For example, they believe that one type of dinosaur became the first bird. Creationists see change as limited, with separate kinds existing from the beginning.

We admit that our belief in creation by God is faith. But since evolution cannot be proven it is a faith, too Since our beliefs come from the Bible, from God Himself we know, without proof, that what God tells us about creation is really true.

63

To Change or Not To Change

The question of change, and evolution, is mainly a question of biology. A review of the important beliefs about biological change will help us to see how important this question is in biology.

Darwin's Challenge

Darwin was not the first to challenge this idea. But he was certainly the most effective. When he left on his five-year world cruise in 1832, he had no idea he was about to make history. He was simply the ship's naturalist, and he made careful study of plant and animal life all along the way. On the way the ship stopped in the Galapagos Islands off the west coast of South America.

The Galapagos are a cluster of islands, each with its own plants and animals. Each island, for example, has a slightly different variety of finch. These small, dull birds are not very beautiful. But they were the key in starting Darwin's theory of evolution. Darwin found 13 varieties of finch on the islands, classifiable into two groups: insect-eaters with long, sharp beaks and plant-eaters with strong, blunt beaks for cracking seeds.

Darwin found similar shades of difference among other creatures on the islands. Each island had its own variety of tortoise, each similar to each other and yet different enough that sailors who visited the islands could tell which tortoise came from which island.

"Natural" Selection

When Darwin returned home he began to breed pigeons to see how much variety he himself could produce. All tame varieties of pigeons have come from a single wild species. This shows how much change can occur within a single species. Darwin was amazed to discover that the *breeds* of pigeon differ from each other more than do many *families* of birds in the wild!

If a breeder can produce changes by selecting which plants and animals may reproduce, Darwin thought, perhaps nature can do the same. But how does nature produce a new strain without direction? In the wild the weak die out. If an animal develops something that helps it to live better in its surroundings, that animal survives longer than others and produces more offspring with the same good features. We could say nature has "selected" those features.

Darwin coined the term "natural selection" for the ways in which the unfit are eliminated. If selection were to continue long enough, he thought, any animal could be changed into a new kind of animal. A bear could be changed into a whale, he once wrote.

The fixed, stable view of nature was replaced by a view of the world as constantly shifting and changing.

Clusters and Gaps

But had Darwin gotten carried away with his idea? Both creation scientists and many evolutionary scientists point out that living things cannot be arranged in a continuous, unbroken series from simplest to most complex. Instead we find *groups* of similar animals, separated from other groups by definite *gaps*.

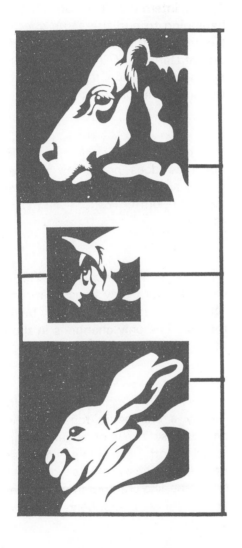

This is why we can easily tell one plant or animal from another. For example, it is easy to tell the difference between animals as similar as horses, cows, sheep, and goats. Even though they are a lot alike, no one would say these animals were identical, or that they merge with one another. No one would confuse horses with cows, or be unable to tell where horses end and cows begin.

The same situation is true for the fossil record of once-living things. The fossils don't show a smooth range of living creatures blending from one type to another. Many famous evolutionary scientists have also admitted that this same thing is true for the fossil record. The fossils tell us that there have always been clear-cut differences between different kinds of animals.

Any biological theory about change must deal with this fact that there are separate kinds of animals living today, and that these separate kinds of animals remain separate kinds in the fossil record.

Both the indirect scientific evidence which we find in the fossil record, as well as the direct scientific evidence in living things support the Biblical statements that living things reproduce after their kinds.

The Moths In England

One of the most popular "evidences" for evolution is the change in population of the light and dark peppered moths of England. In the past, there were a large number of the light-colored moths. They blended well against the lichen growing on the trees, so their light coloring was a protection against being seen and eaten by birds. Through the years, as industry spewed out more and more pollution, the lichen were killed and the tree trunks darkened. Now it was no longer a protection to be light-colored. The light-colored moths showed up against the darker tree trunks, and the population decreased as birds began to pick them off.

There is also a darker variety of the same moth. There had been fewer dark moths up to this time since they were more easily seen by birds. Now, however, their dark color blended against the dark trees and their numbers increased.

This shows the built-in genetic ability which organisms have in order to adapt to their environment. But does it prove evolution? Does it show the large-scale, new, upward changes necessary for evolutionary progress? Has anything new developed?

However the populations may change from light to intermediate to dark, they remain from beginning to end the same species of moth. Noting this, the introduction to the 1971 edition of Darwin's *Origin of Species* denies that the moths demonstrate evolution in action. Consider the following:

No large-scale change: The change observed does not cross the gap between moths and any other insect. It does not lead to bees or butterflies, or even to a new species of moth!

No new characterictics: The dark moths existed before they became more numerous. The darker color is already built in to the moths. The only change is in the *proportion* of dark moths in the population.

No increase in complexity: Color change is merely a change in the population without new genes. The wing is still a wing, the moth is still a moth. The changes required for evolution — turning a reptile's leg into a bird's wing or an ape-like creature into a human being — would be a completely different order of change.

See also "Galapagos"

66

Scientists describe what living things *do*. They breathe, eat, move, reproduce, and give off waste products. But it is much harder to pinpoint what life *is*.

The question of how life began is an important topic of debate. The more we understand what life is, the clearer becomes the question of whether life came from nonliving matter.

As the science of biology has grown, so has our knowledge of living things. Today we know that there is no such thing as a simple cell. Each living cell is a wonder of purpose and design. A living cell produces chemicals more complex than even our best scientists can make in their laboratories!

God can be called the greatest scientist of all, because not only did He so wonderfully design the inner workings of life, but He is the Designer of all that we study in science. His greatest Design is the plan of salvation by grace, through faith in Jesus Christ.

Nature's "First Tries"

The early evolutionists did not think the origin of life was much of a problem. They looked through their microscopes at tiny bacteria and one-celled animals and it seemed to them that here, certainly, were the simplest possible forms of life. They seemed to be barely alive. What was a cell, after all, but merely an outer skin with a kind of jelly (protoplasm) inside? It contained nothing more complex than a small speck in the center and a few holes scattered through the jelly.

Life

What is it?

The step from nonliving chemicals to these simple blobs seemed a small one and easy to cross.

Small is Not Simple

Small, however, is not simple. A miniature computer is not less complicated than a large one. It may even be more complicated. One-celled organisms came under careful study as supposed "missing links" between life and nonlife. It soon became clear that they are not just blobs of jelly. In fact, they are perhaps *more* amazing than the higher animals, because they carry on the same functions of life without the organs we have. They don't have stomachs, but they digest food; they don't have lungs, but they take in oxygen; they don't have kidneys or bladders, but

67

they collect uric acid in packets and expel it.

The scientific word for one-celled organisms is "protozoa," meaning "pre-animal." Yet they are not at all pre-animals, but are in every way truly animals. There are at least fifteen or twenty thousand different kinds of protozoa, which are very different from each other.

The greatest problem for the theory of evolution is *not* how modern living things came from the original one-celled creatures. It is rather how simple chemicals crossed the great gulf to complex one-celled living things. The difference between nonliving chemicals and the simplest forms of life *is much greater* than the difference between a single-celled creature and the horse.

Evolutionists once thought it would be easy to explain the evolution of one-celled creatures. But now that we know how complex they are, one-celled creatures are as hard to explain as a man or an elephant.

Life Means Chemical Order

How many of you would answer that life is *order*? Life is the highest level of order of anything in the universe. For example, your own body is made up of about 60,000,000,000,000 tiny cells. Each one of those cells is like a large network of factories. There are "factories" for making food, and there are "warehouses" for storing it. There are factories for burning oxygen, and there are ways of getting rid of waste material.

All of this depends on order. And it is not simple at all. If only one "factory" in one of the cells does not work correctly, that cell would soon die.

The living cell is a tiny industrial complex, carefully balanced and timed — all packed into a space so small you cannot even see it!

Where Did This Order Come From

Living things are systems of orderly mechanisms. The question of how life began is really the question of how such a high level of order came to be.

For centuries most people have thought that the order in life was proof that the universe was the product of intelligent creation. To use an example, imagine you are walking along the beach and find a watch in the sand. How many of you would exclaim, "Look what the ocean made"? We all know that it takes planning and intelligence to make a watch. There is no evidence that the physical world can do the intelligent planning to create a machine by itself. This is the position taken by creationists today.

Evolutionists, however, feel that they can explain life by using just the laws of nature. They believe that natural forces in the world itself must have created the ordered systems of life. Without any outside help, a mix of chemicals developed into an organized living system. They believe just by chance chemicals were lined up in the right order and that these chemicals began working together in the first living systems. At every following step of evolution life became more ordered, more organized, more coordinated by natural forces alone.

The evolutionary explanation for the origin of life tries to replace the intelligent design and power of God with the workings of natural forces.

THE SOURCE OF ORDER

What does it take to make a living cell alive? None of the parts that make up the cell is alive. Not one of the molecules within the cell is itself alive. But when all those parts are in the right places in the right amounts, working in the right way at the right time — the cell lives.

In this way the living cell is no different from machines made by humans. What makes an airplane fly? None of its parts fly on their own. The wings won't fly all by themselves. They need engines. But the engines don't fly by themselves either.

The airplane flies because of the way its parts are put together, its organization. In the same way, life is a result of organization. We cannot explain the origin of life unless we can discover a source of its organization.

The source of all the order in the universe is God. Read Genesis 1:2. Here we see that at first the heavens and the earth were in disorder. But God's activity, begining with the creation of light on the first day, began to order everything until, at the end of the sixth day, God saw all that He had made, and it was very good.

WHAT ARE THE CHANCES FOR LIFE?

Imagine the newspaper headlines if scientists ever did create life. They may, in fact, some day do so. Science has repeatedly done more than people thought it could.

Yet, even if scientists did create life, would that prove that life originally came from an ancient chemical "stew" by chance? Not at all. Nobody tries to create life from matter and energy alone. Nobody places the simple chemicals of life in a mixer, hoping to get life. Scientists spend lots of money and hours studying, planning and testing. These scientific activities show that it takes a lot of intelligence, work and energy to organize matter *toward* life.

Man's best efforts have not been able to create life. Surely chance could not do it. But God created life very easily, and on an awesome scale. These human efforts are good scientific demonstrations that God created the heavens and the earth and everything in them.

Even modern biology teaches us what the Bible has told people for thousands of years — life was created by God Himself. There is no other explanation for life.

Those who want to believe in an explanation for life which removes God, have put a lot of faith in the "creation of life" experiments. People put their faith in something. God invites us to trust His promises of forgiveness in Jesus Christ.

See also "Design"

Oceanography

The Study of Our Oceans

As it sweeps through space our planet earth looks like a giant blue marble swirled with white. It is the huge oceans that make it look blue, and the white is from the clouds.

The oceans of the earth are all connected, so they could be thought of as one big ocean. They cover 70% of the earth's surface, about 140,000,000 square miles. People who live inland and who do not get out on the ocean may not realize just how big it is.

The volume of water in the oceans is so large it is hard to imagine. The oceans contain about 316 million CUBIC MILES of water. A cubic mile is a cube with each edge one mile long. Try imagining a cube this size. Think about this: ALL of the people in the WORLD,

about 5 billion of them, could be easily packed into ONE cubic mile, with space left over! Each cubic mile of water contains about 1,101,187,900,000 gallons of water. Can you read this number? There is a lot of water in the oceans!

More water is being added to the oceans every year. Where does it come from? Scientists have recently found that the earth's heat is forcing water out of rocks in the earth's crust. This water enters the oceans through volcanoes and undersea hot springs. As much as 430 million tons of water each year may be added to the oceans in this manner. So there is no shortage of water on the earth, even though it might not be easy to convince people who live in the desert of this.

Sometimes people wonder if there is enough water to flood the earth all over as the Bible claims happened to Noah. You can be sure there is enough water. If the earth were a smooth sphere, that is, all the mountains flattened out and the sea bottoms raised, the waters of the oceans would cover the earth to a depth of 12,000 feet! That is more than two **miles**. You can be sure that a worldwide flood with water that deep would be able to make great changes on the surface of the earth. Creationists believe this is just what happened, and that today's world is very different from what it was before Noah's Flood.

Here are some interesting facts about each of the world's great oceans: The PACIFIC OCEAN, with an area of 63,800,000 square miles, is the world's largest, covering over one-third of the world's surface. Its average depth is about 14,000 feet, and the deepest spot is the Challenger Deep, southwest of Guam, at 36,198 feet. This is deeper than Mt. Everest is tall!

The ATLANTIC OCEAN is the second largest, with an area of 31,530,000 square miles. It has the same average depth as the Pacific.

I told you three guys over and over . . . dinosaurs go in the middle.

Its deepest spot is the Milwaukee Deep, north of Puerto Rico, at 27,498 feet. The North Atlantic can be very stormy with waves 40 feet and more.

The INDIAN OCEAN is third, with an area of 28,356,000 square miles and an average depth of 13,000 feet. Its deepest spot is 25,000 feet, south of the island of Java.

The ARCTIC and ANTARCTIC OCEANS are harder to define. The Arctic Ocean surrounds the North Pole, with an area of 5,440,000 square miles. It is only about 5000 feet deep on the average, with the deepest spot going down to 18,880 feet and is mostly ice-covered. The Antarctic Ocean surrounds the continent of Antarctica, and some authorities simply consider it the "bottoms" of the Atlantic, Pacific, and Indian Oceans.

The water itself that fills these oceans is very special stuff. We think of water as very common and unexciting. But liquid water is very rare in our solar system, and maybe in the whole universe. (Most other water is either frozen or steam on other planets.) Water has many special properties that make creationists think it was designed for life on earth and is not just an accident. Here is a list of special things about water:

(1) Water is liquid at ordinary temperatures found on earth.

(2) Water can absorb more heat than anything except ammonia.

(3) Water expands when it freezes, so ice floats.

(4) Water has high surface tension.

(5) Water has capillary action.

(6) Water can dissolve almost anything, if given enough time.

(7) Water lets light pass through it very well.

All these features of water are important. (2) allows water to help regulate the earth's climate. (3) means that ice floats: what would happen if it didn't? (4) means water pulls its surface tight like a drumhead. (5) means water can climb up narrow tubes and soak into things. (6) means water is the solvent, or carrier, for a lot of chemical solutions. The most important to you right now is your blood! (7) allows plant life to grow in the sea, as well as letting sea animals see where they're swimming. Creationists think all these things about water show that it was designed as a special substance by a Creator God.

Lastly, we need to think about the ocean bottoms. For a long time, scientists had no way to tell what the deep ocean floors looked like; they thought the ocean bottoms were fairly flat and featureless. But during World War II, SONAR (SOound Navigation And Ranging) echo-sounding was developed, and "pictures" of the underwater landscape emerged. Instead of being flat and blah, the oceans hid mighty mountain ranges, deep trenches, steep-walled canyons and towering volcanos, matching anything on the continents. Any good encyclopedia will show you a picture of the "underwater moonscape."

One of the most impressive and important features underwater is the Mid-Atlantic Ridge. This is a 40,000-mile-long, 1000-mile-wide, winding chain of undersea volcanic mountains as large and rough as the Rockies. It winds around under the Atlantic Ocean and through the Indian Ocean. It looks like a big surgical scar, as if once the earth broke open there.

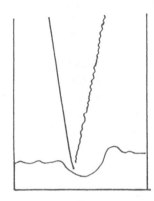

SONAR

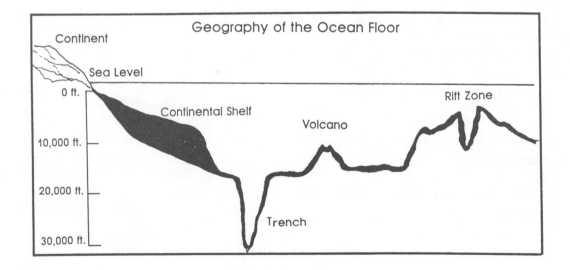

Geography of the Ocean Floor

We want to conclude this   with a look at the importance of the oceans to man, some of their possibilities, and speculate about their future.

Here are the main services and resources of the oceans to man:

(1) **Climatic Thermostat** — The great heat-absorbing capacity of water, along with the 70-30% water/land distribution, helps keep the air from warming up or cooling off too fast. This keeps the climate liveable over most of the earth; otherwise, there would be temperature extremes, and violent winds and storms.

(2) **Oxygen Generator** — We said before that plankton produce oxygen. They produce **most** of the world's oxygen, to renew the portion used up by animal breathing and fires. It would be very serious if a large chemical spill would kill plankton over a large area of the sea. For this reason alone, man cannot afford to pollute the ocean.

(3) **Rain Reservoir** — The oceans supply the water for rainfall, as the power of sunlight distills (evaporates) water into the atmosphere from them. They get the water back from rivers that drain the land. The importance c

rainfall should be obvious; the land areas would become total deserts without it, and nothing could live.

(4) **Food Source** — Many of the oceans' animals are edible by man. The amount of food in the sea could feed all the world's population well, and then some. But man has not yet learned to farm and harvest the sea properly. Some species, especially the whales, are in danger of dying out. Sea farming has to be done so as to avoid reducing animals' numbers too much or creating pollution. It can be done, but it has not been done.

(5) **Mineral Resource** — Nodules of manganese the sea floor, and there are deposits of gold and silver and many other valuable minerals in the ocean, either dissolved in the water, or on or under the bottom. Man can learn to mine the seas, too. Some of these minerals have been washed off the land. As they become more scarce on land sources, the ocean minerals will become more and more important.

(6) **Energy Source** — It is possible, at least in theory, to use the force of waves and tides to generate electricity. This is a way of using solar power secondhand, and gravity-power in the case of tides. There is at least one water power station in France that is run by trapped tide waters. If wave power can be harnessed, it would do much to solve man's need for pollution-free electrical energy.

only hope they will not create damage.

(7) Living Space — There is plenty of room in the sea, for people, too, if they can devise ways of living there. Many land areas on earth are not very pleasant or easy places to live. But there are large coastal areas where shallow underwater living might be possible. Special underwater buildings must be made to do this, but it may not be as difficult as going to the moon. It would be easier and more profitable to build undersea colonies than to colonize the moon or Mars.

These, then, are the major areas of importance of the oceans. Scientists now know that any serious upset of ocean system life will eventually have an impact on land animals and man. Man has in the past used the oceans as his garbage dump. Many dangerous chemicals have been ''disposed of'' there. We can

The oceans are great, living, self-renewing systems that can bestow great blessings on mankind. But it all depends on how man uses them, if he will follow the command God gave him in the garden of Eden. Otherwise, if man destroys the oceans, he will destroy himself in the process.

Knowing these facts, Christians should work to promote protection and respect for the world's oceans and the God-created life they sustain. The first oceanographer (ocean scientist) was a strong Christian who rejected evolution. Because of this, God blessed his scientific study, and today Matthew Maury is a well-known scientist of the past. If we follow his Christian example in science, God will also bless our study and use of the oceans!

Oil spills, along with the dumping of industrial waste, have had far-reaching harmful effects on life in the ocean.

Petroleum

CRUDE OIL. Another name for petroleum is crude oil.

CRUDE OIL is oil as it comes from the ground. CRUDE OIL is not like the oil you see at the store. It is usually very black and thick. It flows slowly like honey. Oil, gasoline, and many other things are made from CRUDE OIL.

CRUDE OIL must be REFINED. This means that it is heated in big towers to separate the gasoline from the oil and other liqiuds in CRUDE OIL.

WHERE DOES OIL COME FROM?

What would life be like today without petroleum? We depend on gasoline to run our cars. But we make many other things from it, too. We make plastics and medicines from petroleum. Much of our electricity is made by power plants which burn oil or natural gas. Natural gas is also made when petroleum is made in the earth.

At one time evolutionists thought that petroleum took millions of years to form. But creation scientists said that the world was not that old.

Today oil scientists know that petroleum can be made quickly. It does not take millions of years to make it. Oil has been made in a very short time from water and plant materials in the laboratory. At least one company, Pyrenco, sells a machine which makes fuel from plant waste in 20 minutes! It is used mostly on farms.

We are also learning that petroleum is made much more rapidly in nature than we thought. It has been found forming in ooze located at the bottom of the Gulf of Mexico. It would seem that petroleum is being generated even as you read these words!

The Bible's history of the world says that the world is about 6,000 years old. Scientists who believe the Bible knew that oil did not take millions of years to make. They always knew the Bible was right.

Our world is very concerned about oil today. This means that we think a lot about energy sources like coal and petroleum. How are coal and oil formed? There are two major views of how coal and oil are formed in the earth. The evolutionary view says that oil and coal formed over millions of years, through slow processes. The creationist, young earth view says that coal and oil are made quickly.

The word petroleum means *rock oil*. Although petroleum is usually thought of as a mineral resource, it is not a natural mineral. Even though petroleum is obtained from rock formations, it is a product of once-living things. Chemists have been able to make petroleum by applying heat and pressure to ooze taken from the ocean.

Creation scientists who accept the truth of Scripture about their salvation know that the Bible is true. They know that it is also true when it says that God made all things, including oil. They are studying to learn how God might have made oil.

PETROLEUM AND THE FLOOD

Many creation scientists believe that petroleum, like coal, is the result of a worldwide flood. Plant life in the seas grew very well in the warm climate before the flood. When they died, they sank to the bottom and made a lot of ooze. This is how oil starts.

We have all seen the thick muck which is sometimes found at the bottom of lakes. This muck, also found at the bottom of the oceans, is made of the decaying remains of plants and animals. According to evolutionary theory, there were big collections of this muck on ocean bottoms millions of years ago. These deposits were incredibly huge.

Silt from rocks settled out of the water onto the muck. This caused pressure on the muck layer. This pressure caused heat to build up. This caused a chemical change in the muck which made the oil we know today.

This silt continued to build up over millions of years, according to evolutionists. The silt hardened into rocks many feet deep over the oil. But the oil was still free to move below the earth's surface, as water does.

Over the years movements in the earth's rocks locked much of the petroleum in place. This is where we find it today. This is why oil geologists often look for certain types of formations in the earth's crust which may contain the locked-in oil. When they find oil in such formations, it does not prove that the earth is millions of years old.

Geologists who believe what the Bible says about the earth's history know that oil was made by God since the creation of the world. The world is only about 6,000 years old, according to the Bible. Can oil be older than 6,000 years old?

Oil starts out as very tiny droplets which are made in the ooze. Since oil floats on water, the tiny drops of oil, made in water and plant ooze, would float to the highest point under the water that they could find. When enough of them would collect in some underground pool, they would float to a new place under the rocks. Finally, many pools of oil would collect into an even bigger pool.

These pools of oil would find even more pools forming from the ooze and join them. Soon you would have the giant underground pools of oil we know of today.

Creation scientist Dr. Henry Morris has studied oil. He has found that oil in the earth can move much more quickly than evolutionists used to think. This means that oil collection within the earth happens rapidly. He also points out that the evolutionary explanation for the formation of oil means nothing to the actual search for oil. Many people do not know that oil geologists do not need the evolutionary explanation in order to know where to find oil.

Oil and coal, which have given us the kind of world we know today, are wonderful gifts from God. He knew we needed these things before we did!

See also "Coal"

78

Science

SCIENCE — WHAT IS IT?

Man has always wanted to know about the world in which he lives and has tried to learn about it. We are very curious.

Science is a special way of studying the world in which we live. It is a way of organizing what we learn about the world. Science is not a difficult subject. Each of us uses science every day.

For example, let us say that you have to clean some windows. You have a choice of what you might use to clean the windows: vegetable oil, or water with a little ammonia and soap in it. You know that the vegetable oil simply won't work. But you also know that the soap and water **should** work well. Maybe you even know that the ammonia will help keep the window from streaking. This is an example of a basic knowledge of chemistry in action.

When God created man He told us to ''subdue'' the earth. This very literally means that we are to make the things of the creation serve our needs. But in order to do this, we need to learn about the creation and the principles which God created. This Biblical command is what science is all about.

The Scientific Method

Let's use a simple problem to illustrate the scientific method. Let's experimentally test the common idea that fish need air in order to live. This will show us the scientific method.

STEP 1 — The Statement of the Problem, in this case, "Can it be proven that fish require air to breathe, even though they live under water."

STEP 2 — The Experiment. The scientific method requires that we prove the facts about this first-hand. To do this we will need **two** aquariums. We fill both aquariums with water, fish and enough special food (which will not foul the water), and seal them up air-tight. The second aquarium will be our **control**. The second aquarium will have one additional thing that the first does not: a small air hose bubbling air into the water, and a small hole on top for the air to escape. The experiment requires that we keep careful records of everything we do, and everything we see.

STEP 3 — Forming the hypothesis. Once we have all the results of our experiment, we can form a hypothesis—an explanation for what we have seen in the experiment. The fish in the tank without air died. The fish in the tank with air lived. Why?

STEP 4 — Testing the hypothesis. In order to prove whether our hypothesis is true, we must now test it. If, after more testing, our hypothesis still stands up we can offer a **theory**: "Fish require air, dissolved in the water, in order to live."

In John chapter 7 we see where some people were drawing some conclusions about Jesus and what He was doing without really checking facts to see if their conclusions were right. So Jesus says, in John 7:24, "Do not judge according to appearance, but judge with righteous judgment." Is it important to have all the facts?

YOU ARE A SCIENTIST!

Science is not as mysterious as it sounds. Let's take an example of a situation in which you probably didn't even know that you were acting as a scientist. Let's say that you are having a picnic out in the back yard one Saturday afternoon. The washing is done and hung out to dry. The windows of your house are open to let the warm breeze in. And your picnic is spread out on the lawn. What a beautiful day!

All of a sudden the sun disappears. You look up and see that you are surrounded by thick black clouds. Almost at the same time that you notice this, a cold gust hits your face, and the sky starts to rumble. Then you see lightenings streaking closer and closer through the sky. What is going on? What will happen next?

Of course, you say, it's probably going to rain. You would start packing up your picnic, get the clothes in, and close the windows. And you would probably hurry!

This has happened to all of us many times. But you probably never thought that you were acting as a scientist in this situation. All the elements of science were present in what you experienced. You collected information: there were dark clouds, cool wind, thunder and lightening. You then decided on a theory: it is going to rain! This theory also happens to be a prediction, which is another part of science.

Science is not mysterious at all. Consider the example above—where would we be without science? The organization that science brings to our thinking helps us to sort out what would otherwise be a very confusing world. Scientists today often explore more difficult problems, but the principle is the same.

It is also pretty obvious that science in and of itself is not against the Bible. In fact, if we are to take God's command to subdue the earth seriously, we need some sort of method like the scientific method. If we are careful in our study of science, and our study of the Bible, we will glorify God in the process!

See also "Scientists"

81

Scientists

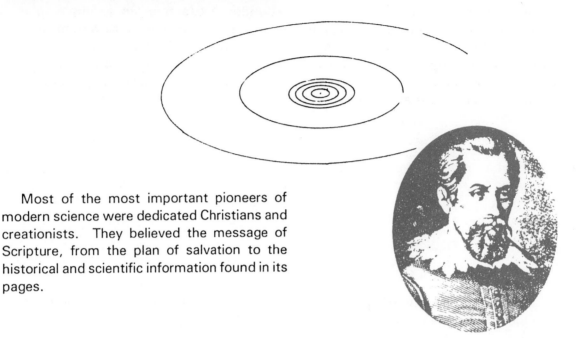

Most of the most important pioneers of modern science were dedicated Christians and creationists. They believed the message of Scripture, from the plan of salvation to the historical and scientific information found in its pages.

Francis Bacon

Francis Bacon lived from 1561 to 1626 and served as the Lord Chancellor of England. He set up the modern scientific method. In doing this he said that true science must be based on observation and reliable information. Things in science had to be learned firsthand, through experiment. His approach to science changed the way people looked at knowledge about the world. He also started the Royal Society of London.

Sir Francis Bacon was a strong believer in Scripture as the true guide for history as well as saving faith in the Savior. He wrote that since the fall into sin we especially need to concentrate on faith in the Savior.

Johann Kepler

Johann Kepler is usually considered to be the father of modern astronomy (the study of the stars). He built upon the work of others and he used Galileo's telescope. But he began the science of the movements of bodies in space. Now that we are flying in space, his science is especially important to us. He showed that the earth goes around the sun.

Kepler studied Biblical ages and came to the conclusion that the world had been created about 7,000 years ago. He called astronomers ''priests of God,'' who should be careful to give God all the glory He deserves.

Blaise Pascal

Blaise Pascal lived from 1623 to 1662. He was a great mathematician and is considered to be the founder of the science of flowing liquids. He also invented the barometer.

Pascal's Law, which he formulated, is the basis for all hydraulic equipment. Today's heavy equipment especially depends on this principle.

One of the personal treasures of his life is now on display at France's Bibliotheque Nationale, a handwritten record of his conversion to Christianity.

Robert Boyle

Robert Boyle lived from 1627 to 1691. He was one of the founders of the Royal Society of London. He was one of the fathers of modern chemistry. He also made many contributions in physics. He invented an improved air pump which he used to study air. In 1662 he announced what is now called Boyle's Law, which is used to describe how gases act. He also showed that oxygen was the part of the air which supports fire and life.

As a Christian Boyle gave much of his own money to pay people to translate the Bible into new languages for mission work. He also gave money to be used for lectures which defended Biblical religion.

Nicholas Steno

Nicholas Steno was born Nils Stennsen in 1631 and he lived to the year 1686.

In Steno's day most people, including scientists, felt that fossils were simply rocks which looked like living things. Steno came to the conclusion that fossils are actually the mineralized remains of once-living things. He believed that most of the fossils and rock layers could be easily explained by a worldwide flood.

Steno was a deeply religious man and he finally went to work fulltime in the church.

Sir Isaac Newton

Sir Isaac Newton (1642-1727) made many discoveries. He explained how gravity works. He also explained the principles of motion. He also offered the first theory about what light really is. In doing this work he discovered that white light is made up of the colors of the rainbow.

Newton discovered that an object at rest will remain at rest unless some outside force acts upon it. He also found that an object in motion will tend to remain in motion unless acted upon by a force. Today we consider these laws basic and simple, but they had never before been explained.

Newton was also a very active Bible student, and wrote many books on Scripture. His books show that this great scientist believed the Bible: that the earth was created in about 4,000 B.C., in a time of six days, by God.

Louis Pasteur

Louis Pasteur was born in 1822. When he died in 1895 the world was much different—and most of it was his doing. His work has probably saved more lives than the work of any other human being.

He discovered that most illnesses are caused by microscopic creatures. This is called the **germ theory of disease**. As he learned more about the microscopic world of life he also discovered ways in which inoculations could protect man and animals from germ-produced diseases. On July 6, 1885, he inoculated, and saved the first child from rabies.

Another result of his work in this area is **pasteurization**, a method for ridding milk and various other foods from harmful bacteria so that they are safe to drink.

He also showed that life cannot arise from non-life. Life must come from life. People had believed that life could come all by itself until his day. At first scientists who believed in evolution, which says that life did happen all by itself, did not accept him. But he was such a careful scientist that they finally had to believe him.

Pasteur had deep Christian faith. He was against the idea of the evolution of life because it is against the Bible, and because evolution is against science.

LOUIS PASTEUR, PHOTOGRAPHED IN 1884 WHEN HE WAS 61 YEARS OLD. (*Courtesy, Pasteur Institute, Paris.*)

See also "Science"

SPACE EXPLORATION — A LEAP FOR MANKIND

"That's one small step for man, one giant leap for mankind!"

These words have become world-famous. They were first spoken by astronaut Neil Armstrong when, at 10:56 p.m. Eastern Daylight Time, July 20, 1969, he became the first person to set foot on the moon.

The Flag is raised at one of our moon bases. You can also see the Lunar Lander and the Lunar Rover, a car which was used to travel to various sites on the moon. *(Courtesy NASA)*

MOON GEOLOGY

When astronaut Neil Armstrong first set foot on the moon, scientists listened to every word: "The surface is fine and powdery. I only go in a small fraction of an inch, maybe an eighth of an inch, but I can see the footprints in the fine sandy particles. There seems to be no difficulty in moving around.... It's a very soft surface, but here and there...I run into a very hard surface... It has a stark beauty like much of the high desert of the United States."

During their historic visit at Tranquillity Base, the astronauts carefully gathered handfuls of moon rocks and scoops of soil. They were put into individual packages and placed in specially sealed containers. They would be studied on earth.

Life on the Moon?

In the early stages of the Apollo program, there were fears that the astronauts and their samples might pick up infecting germs from the moon. So they were temporarily placed in isolation chambers when they returned to earth. But the moon rocks were found to be completely empty of life. Confidence in that fact was so great that after the third Apollo landing, the quarantine period was dropped.

The lack of water and life on the moon was a disappointment to many scientists. They had hoped to find some evidence to support the natural evolution of life.

Evolutionary scientists admitted that none of the rock or soil samples that have been returned show any evidence that there is or ever was life on the moon. One scientist wrote, "This was a disappointment to those advocating widespread life in the universe."

Evolutionary hopes were also destroyed when none of the elements for life could be found. There is not even any oxygen on the moon.

We conclude with the following taken from the book The Moon, Its Creation, Form, and Significance by John Whitcomb and Donald DeYoung:

"One cannot help but reflect on the extreme differences between the comfortable earth and its important but entirely inhospitable satellite companion. If the earth were without its protective atmosphere and abundant water supply, the terrestrial environment would be similar to that of the moon!"

This book, which Apollo astronaut James Irwin recommends for reading, goes on to say, "The contrast of the moon, or of the planets, provides a vivid demonstration of God's care in providing a beautiful earth."

TO SPACE AND BACK

"What goes up must come down."

Until the space age this saying was always true. The first rockets to go into space launched satellites and other spacecraft which never returned to earth. This waste of machinery made space flight very expensive. But since April 1981, the space program has taken a new turn with the flight of the first space shuttle. It takes off like a rocket and lands like an airplane on a runway. Even the rockets are returned to earth on football-field-sized parachutes to be picked up in the Atlantic Ocean by recovery ships.

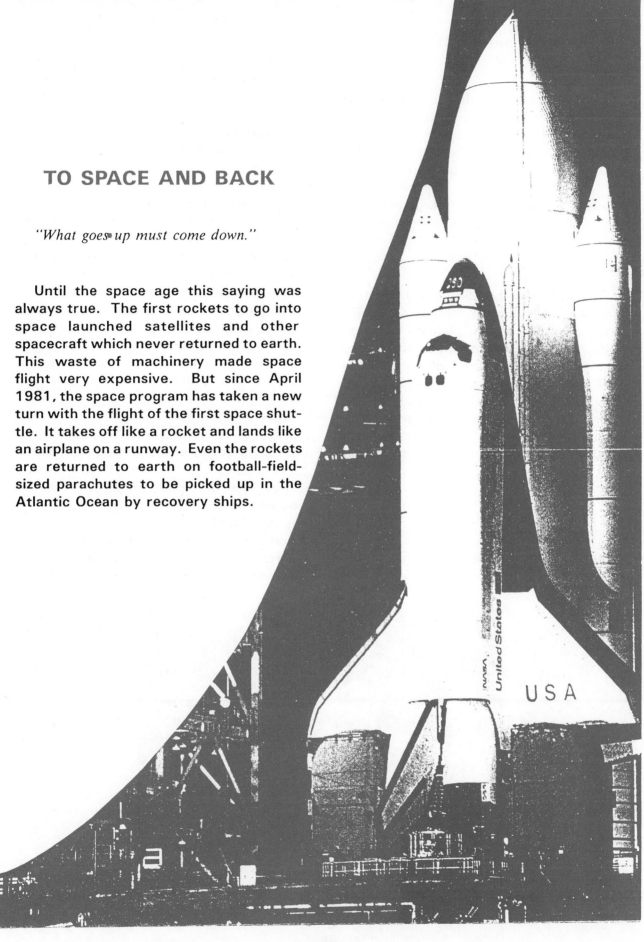

More Shuttle Uses

NASA has already offered free shuttle space to companies that make medicines. They want to try to make very pure medicines which cannot easily be made in gravity. One example is the cancer-fighting hormone interferon. Space can be practical for the making of large amounts of medicines in more pure form than possible on earth.

By the end of the 1980's, shuttle missions could be a weekly routine. Of the 40 or so shuttle flights planned through 1985, about a third are scheduled to carry military payloads. Although the shuttle itself would not be used to fight in space, it will allow the Defense Department to put military satellites into orbit more easily than with rockets. The shuttle will also be able to carry larger things into space.

Space Stations

American space scientists have now turned their attention to orbiting space stations. In 1973 they launched Skylab, an experimental space station that fell to earth in 1979. The shuttle was another step in that direction. The space shuttles will serve as the system of travel between space stations and earth.

The stage is now set for the building of permanent stations in orbit. They will probably be divided into sections so additions can be made to the basic station even after it has been placed in orbit. Artificial gravity could be created by swinging the station like a pendulum counterbalanced by a spent rocket-booster stage connected by long cables. Large solar cell arrays or a nuclear power system would provide electric power.

Space stations will make it possible to set up factories in space which will pay for themselves. The benefits we already have from the use of space (*e.g.* weather satellites) will be greatly increased when professionals can actually make observations from space stations. Geologists, agricultural experts, and oceanographers can do much of their work right in space!

(Courtesy NASA)

Any Earthly Good?

Some people have questioned the use of billions of dollars for space. Could the money would be better spent directly benefitting people here on earth? In fact, there are many ways that peoples' lives on earth have been greatly improved by the results of the space program. Things used in space have also found countless uses in medicine, factories, and science.

With the the space shuttle and space stations, we can stress the practical earthly uses even more. Although scientists are interested in the possibility of using a space station for more exploration of the moon and deep space, the main focus is on products for use on earth.

Satellites are already being used by Christian broadcasters to beam the Gospel to places which could never be reached before. And one of the most prized possessions in distant lands is the gift of cheap pocket radios, made possible by microelectronics used first in space, to pick up these broadcasts. In more modern lands Christian television makes use of communications satellites far out in space. Space *can* be used for the glory of God!

In Job 26:7 we read about what the earth looks like in space! Does this description match the picture on this page? Is the Bible as "up-to-date" as our space age?

Woodpecker

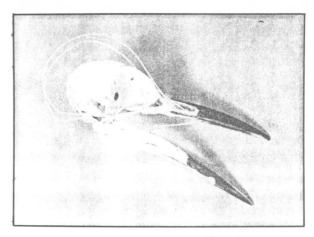

Design in Woodpeckers

from material provided by Luther D. Sunderland

The woodpecker has a number of specially designed features which are special among birds. These features permit it to perform its tasks as a living jackhammer. One of the most amazing features is a tongue that extends three-to-five times the normal length to get worms and insects from hollow trees. One might think it would need to have its tongue rooted in the tail to perform this neat trick. But, the tongue starts in the right nostril. It goes out of the right nostril, splits into two parts, wraps around the skull beneath the skin passing on either side of the neck bones, joins together and comes up through the lower jaw. (See the picture on this page.) The woodpecker's tongue is helped to do this by two special bones called the *hyoid bones*.

As you can see in the picture, two of the hyoid bones exit the right nostril and are connected to the next two bones by miniature ball joints. A third ball joint appears at the fork as it passes through the jaw, where the fifth bone is joined, which stiffens the outer portion of the tongue.

Other special features are:

* a tough beak which can drive through hard wood which would bend a nail;

* strong neck muscles which deliver jackhammer blows to the head and beak;

* a thick skull which withstands continuous shocks that would kill or give a bad headache to other birds;

* a glue factory in the tongue which makes the surface sticky;

* stiff tail feathers with sharp spines which brace the bird for hammering, and viselike toes with two in front and two in back rather than three and one, like all other birds.

How could such a special set of designs like this be the product of chance, ask creation scientists. Think how many millions of robins would need to have bashed their brains out trying to play jackhammer, before not just one, but a pair of them, accidentally got a tongue like that. Even if two were lucky enough to come up with the right tongue, it would have been of no advantage without the other features.

One scientist said while looking at it under a microscope, "It is very easy to tell the difference between man-made and God-made objects. The more you magnify man-made objects, the cruder they look, but the more you magnify God-made objects the more precise and detailed they appear."

See also "Design"

90

IS THE EARTH OLD? —

THE POPULAR VIEW

How old is the earth? If you ask people this question (try it on your friends), you will probably get the answer, "millions of years." You have been told this ever since you could read. If you attended public school, you were told very early that dinosaurs lived millions of years ago. Movies, magazine articles, newspaper articles and TV programs all confidently announce that the earth is old. Not just millions of years, but *billions* of years old. It seems like such a well-established "fact" that few people think about it, much less doubt it.

It is true that the majority of scientists think the world is old. The present estimates are about 4-6 billion years, but there is some disagreement on this. It is *not* true that everybody believes this. There are thousands of creationist scientists who do not, and many more thousands of educated non-scientists who do not, for good reasons. What these scientists say, however, is usually ignored by those who control television, newspapers and the magazines. So people are surprised to hear creationists express the idea that the world is rather young, probably less than 10,000 years old.

In spite of the fact that "everybody" believes that the world is old, the scientific evidence that supports the idea is not very good. In fact, the argument is not over evidence at all. It is over the *meaning* of the evidence. The argument is about the stories scientists make up to explain what happened in the past. Nobody human was around to observe and report how the world began, so we are not dealing with real science here. It is a choice of evolution or of creation.

Scientists did not always believe that the earth was ancient. Those scientists who started modern science were mostly creationists who believed that the earth was young, and they found good scientific evidence to support that idea.

The idea that the earth is very old is fairly new. This idea has been dominant in science for only about 125 years. Up through the 18th century, most scientists and theologians accepted the Bible as true on the question of origins. The earth's history was thought to be short, since the geneologies (family trees) in Genesis were too short to allow for great long ages. The belief in a supernatural beginning of the world, along with a short history up to the present, kept the idea of evolution from being developed and accepted.

It is almost like magic to think time can make impossible or unlikely things happen. It is a kind of faith. Dr. Duane Gish, in his book, **Evolution, The Fossils Say No**, pokes fun at this notion by making up these equations:

$$t = \text{instantaneous}$$

$$\text{Frog} \longrightarrow \text{Prince} = \text{Nursery Tale}$$

$$t = \text{300 million years}$$

$$\text{Frog} \longrightarrow \text{Prince} = \text{Science}$$

has probably never happened, and it is never expected to, because of the way the real world works. You see, we can imagine a lot of things that *could* happen, but never will happen because the world just doesn't work that way.

Here is another example. If you took all the parts of a car and all the tools for assembling them and put them in a big barrel and started

Do you see the problem? Increased time may allow the *chance* for certain things to happen, but that does not increase the likelihood that they will happen at all. Some things that are thought *possible* are so unusual and unlikely that they might as well be called impossible. For example, *could* oxygen move up to the ceiling all at once? If that happened, you would drown in the nitrogen and other gases that make up the air. But such a thing

it turning over and over, after some millions of years you could open the barrel and find a completely assembled and operational car, ready to drive away. You don't believe it? Good. You shouldn't believe evolution, either, for the same reason.

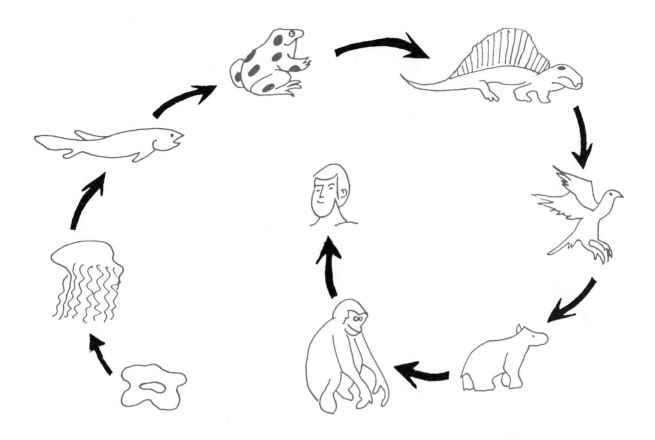

The car is too complex to be assembled by chance. So is your body and that of animals — even plants. But evolutionists want you to believe that chance banging-around of chemical parts over great long ages somehow put together a living cell. And more chance turned it into you. Can you believe that?

What would really happen in the barrel is that everything would be ground into powder long before a million years passed. There is no magic creative power in time alone. Guiding intelligence is necessary to assemble complex machines, living or not. This is what creationists believe. What do you think?

In addition to time, another idea that set the stage for the rise of evolution was called the Chain of Being or the Scale of Nature.

Scientists had noticed that life forms could be arranged in a line, and they became more complicated as they got closer to man. This was an artificial arrangement, and at first it was not thought that one form changed into another, but that God had created all the forms. But this neat arrangement turned out to be handy for evolutionists. All they had to do was develop an argument showing how one life form MIGHT be changed into another, and presto! — instant evolution.

In summary, there are two points to remember. (1) Time was and still is important in making evolutionary theory believable, and (2) the scientific belief in great earth ages does not rest on solid evidence, but developed historically as a reaction against belief in the Bible.

IS THE EARTH OLD —
LET SCIENCE SPEAK

There are many earth-age indicators that give a young age for the world. Dr. Henry Morris in his book, **The Scientific Case For Creation**, lists a table of 70 ways to measure the earth's age on pages 55 to 59. 34% of these give ages less than 10,000 years, and 64% give ages 1,000,000 years or less. This is far below the present evolutionary estimates of 4 to 6 *billion* years. All this disagreement between methods means one thing: they are not very reliable. Dating the earth's rocks is not easy or simple.

We want to look at some scientific situations that suggest the earth is young, instead of old. Think about them and try to remember them so you can share them with others.

(1) The earth has a magnetic field around it. It is probably caused by electric currents deep inside the earth. Careful measurements over a long time show that the magnetic field is getting weaker. It is one-half as strong every 1400 years or so. If you go back in time and double the field's strength every 1400 years, soon the earth's magnetic field would be as strong as a star's. The currents inside would heat up the earth and destroy all life. So the earth must be young.

(2) The earth's rotation speed is slowing down almost one second per year. This cannot have been going on for billions of years, or the earth would have had to be spinning too fast in the beginning. This indicates that the earth cannot be very old.

(3) The sun is shrinking by about five feet per hour. This cannot have been going on for millions of years either, or the starting size of the sun would have been so big it would have burned up the earth.

(4) Natural gas is often found with oil deposits under high temperature and pressure. How fast the gas can escape through the rock can be computed. If the oil and gas are millions of years old, the gas pressure should have dropped to near zero. Why hasn't it? One answer is that these materials were not formed that long ago.

(5) Both the earth and moon sweep up space dust at a rate that can be fairly well estimated. If both are billions of years old, there should be a lot of this dust, which is easy to identify, on the surface. On earth it might be washed into the oceans, but tests do not find it there. On the moon, there is no weather to move it anywhere. It should be hundreds of feet deep, but it is less than an inch deep on the moon. Where is it?

(6) The sun sweeps up space dust like a giant vacuum cleaner. If it is millions of years old, all the tiny dust particles should be gone, clear out to the orbit of Jupiter. But there is a lot of micro-dust near the sun. Why is it still there? Could it be the sun is young?

These are only six evidences[2], from many. They are strictly scientific problems, not religious ones. Evolutionists have not answered them well. Creationists believe they have better answers in the idea of a young earth, supernaturally created, as the Bible teaches. We believe that in time this view will be proved true.

See also "Flood"

Glossary

anthracite: the hardest type of coal.   Anthracite is the result of pressure and heat applied to bituminous coal.

anthropology: the study of man and his civilizations.

Big Bang: the idea that the universe began billions of years ago as a result of a large explosion in space.

bituminous: soft coal which is formed from pressure on lignite.

catastrophism: the idea that the geological changes on the earth have been the result of sudden and violent forces.

creationist: someone who believes that God created all things. Are you a creationist?

Darwin, Charles: the man who popularized the idea that the plants and animals we know today were **not** created by God. He said that they were made from other creatures over long periods of time without God. He is famous for his book which teaches this idea: **Origin of the Species**.

design: the careful and intelligent planning which makes things work.   Houses are **designed**, not just thrown together without a plan.

Doppler effect: the change in the frequency of sound, or light waves, because of the motion source of the sound or light, or the motion of the observer.

ecology: the study of the relationships between plants and animals in the world.

environment: your surroundings, where you live, play and go to school.   Everything around you.

evolution: a slow change from one thing into another thing.

extinct: having stopped living, often used when a whole group of creatures are no longer alive.

fossil: part of a dead plant or animal that has turned to stone when body parts are replaced with minerals dissolved in water.

geological column: the theoretical collection of all the layers of sedimentary rock on earth, stacked, one upon the other, in the order in which they were formed.   The geological column does not exist **anywhere** on earth.

geology: the study of the earth's rocks.   **geologist**: one who studies the earth's rocks.

hypothesis: in science, an untested idea which may or may not be true.

index fossil: a fossil which is usually found only in certain types of rock. Since an index fossil is common only in one or two types of rock, evolutionists use them to tell how old the rock is. (**See "Fossil Record" for the reasons why this method cannot be trusted**.)

kind: each type of animal God created, like dogs. There are many types of dogs in the dog "kind".   One kind can never turn into another kind.

law: in science, an idea which has been carefully tested and studied and found to be always true.

lignite: the softest coal, although technically lignite is not considered true coal. Lignite burns very easily.

macroevolution: large-scale biological change, as in the change from a fish to an amphibian.

microevolution: a small change in the appearance of plants or animals such as in the breeding of dogs. This change has nothing to do with evolution.

natural selection: a term used by evolutionists to describe how animals which evolve become extinct because they are not able find food or protect themselves as well as other animals.

Neanderthal: once presented as evidence for human evolution, Neanderthal man is now considered completely human.

"out-of-place" fossil: a fossil or a man-made object which is found in rock which is "too old" according to evolution. Human footprints found in the same layer of rock as dinosaur footprints are "out-of-place" fossils. According to evolution, dinosaurs became exinct 60 million years before there were people. "Out-of-place" fossils give us evidence that the Biblical history is correct and evolutionary history is in error.

overthrust: a situation in which one layer of rock has slid over the top of another layer due to powerful forces within the earth. Overthrusts always show evidence of the violence of the sliding between the layers involved.

Piltdown man: now recognized as a fraud, this fossil, made up from the jaw of an ape and a human skull, was used as "proof" for human evolution for many years.

red shift: the shifting of light toward the red part of the spectrum, noticed in some light coming from sources far out in space.

satellite: a body in space which moves in orbit around another body. The Moon is the earth's satellite.

spectrum: the colors resulting when white light is separated into its various colors; as seen in a rainbow or light passed through a prism.

solar system: the sun and all the planets around it, including the earth.

theory: in science, an attempt to scientifically describe a range of events and show how they are related. Theories can be disproven as more facts are learned.

transition: (as in "transitional fossil"), any fossil which can be used by evolutionists to show that one kind of animal changed into another kind of animal. No *transitional fossils* are known to exist!

For more information and additional teaching resources, all listed in our up-to-date catalog, free upon request, please write: The Bible-Science Association, 2911 East 42nd Street, Minneapolis, Minneosta, 55406.